T0004626

CLOSER THAN EVER

CLOSER THAN EVER

A Relationship Communication Skills Workbook for Couples

SONYA JENSEN, LMFT

ROCKRIDGE
PRESS

I want to dedicate this book to my amazing partner, Erik. Thank you for following through on your promise to make this life full of adventure. And to all the clients I've worked with who have taught me so much and entrusted their relationships and families to me—I am forever grateful!

Copyright © 2022 by Rockridge Press

All rights reserved. No part of this publication may be reproduced, stored in a retrieval system, or transmitted in any form or by any means, electronic, mechanical, photocopying, recording, scanning, or otherwise, without the prior written permission of the Publisher. Requests to the Publisher for permission should be addressed to the Permissions Department, Rockridge Press, 1955 Broadway, Suite 400, Oakland, CA 94612.

First Rockridge Press trade paperback edition 2022

Rockridge Press and the Rockridge Press logo are trademarks or registered trademarks of Callisto Media Inc. and/or its affiliates in the United States and other countries and may not be used without written permission.

For general information on our other products and services, please contact our Customer Care Department within the United States at (866) 744-2665, or outside the United States at (510) 253-0500.

Paperback ISBN: 978-1-68539-650-3 | eBook ISBN: 978-1-68539-954-2

Manufactured in the United States of America

Interior and Cover Designer: Jami Spittler
Art Producer: Samantha Ulban
Editor: Adrian Potts
Production Editor: Jenna Dutton
Production Manager: Lanore Coloprisco

All images courtesy of © Shutterstock.
Author photo courtesy of Anna Kraft.

10 9 8 7 6 5 4 3 2 1 0

CONTENTS

INTRODUCTION

Welcome! It's an honor and pleasure to share with you the many tools I've learned as a licensed marriage and family therapist, certified Gottman therapist, and certified sex therapist. My motivation and passion is to support couples with clear tools for communication, identify and address underlying issues that keep couples disconnected, and support couples with the words to really express what they want to say.

This workbook is designed to help you understand the common issues that plague couples' ability to communicate effectively and to offer you guidance to see you through it. Nothing in this life is really black and white, and the same is true with relationships. Your differences can become the building blocks of growth in your relationship, or they can become walls between you.

I married my partner when I was very young and with little knowledge of what it meant to build lasting intimacy. My partner was in the military at the time we met, and I saw so many other young couples struggling in the same ways we were. I knew that the field of psychology was my destination, and I wanted answers for real struggles. Since graduate school, I have gone on to do extensive study in couples therapy and what makes love last.

In the early years of my marriage and work, I thought it came down to finding out who was right and who was wrong around a given topic. Since then, I've learned that it's about building a map of each partner's brain, to see how they work separately and together, and to better understand and connect with each other. It is likely that you picked up this workbook because you have a desire to be seen, heard, and accepted for who you are. There is much you can teach your partners, and so much you can learn from them, when curiosity and empathy are attached to your conversations.

Make no mistake, this workbook is not a replacement for seeking treatment for any ongoing debilitating feelings of depression or anxiety. It is a sign of strength to ask for help, and in the Resources section at the back of this book you can find more information about connecting with a therapist. It's also helpful to understand that change in a relationship takes two people with a desire and commitment to put in the work. The tools you will learn in this workbook will be most effective when you and your partner are working on it together.

HOW TO USE THIS BOOK

There are two parts to this workbook. The first part will address the foundational concepts of how to build and maintain healthy communication in a relationship. The second part will focus on the practice of communicating with clear and concise tools. This workbook is highly interactive and designed for you and your partner to complete at the same time. You will find assessments, prompts, exercises, and practices that will stimulate conversations between you and your partner.

The goal of this workbook is to help you understand each other better and not judge each other's differences. Come to this workbook with an open mind and heart, and not a judgmental spirit of whose views and perspective are more correct. If you find it difficult to do this, then I would encourage you to seek support from a therapist while going through this book.

You may not need all the tools in this workbook. Take the ones that are most meaningful for you based on the state of your relationship and the unique issues that you and your partner struggle with. Whether your relationship is in a great place or in need of much support, there are resources available for you in this book to better understand the issues and what topics you need more support on with your partner.

PART I

UNDERSTANDING THE FUNDAMENTALS OF COMMUNICATION

There are foundational concepts that establish what a healthy relationship looks like and the barriers that keep couples from practicing them. Throughout the first part of this book, you will look into what communication in a relationship means, the benefits of healthy communication, understanding each of your communication styles, and so much more.

This first part is meant to be an overview to prepare you for the tools that will come in part 2 of the workbook. Take your time to process and talk with each other about what you're learning, and identify which aspects of communication you do well in together as well as the areas where you may need more support. A couple can benefit from learning new tools and developing awareness and understanding throughout every stage of their relationship. No one has a perfect relationship, and in these pages, you will find that there is hope and clarity for every step of your journey as a couple.

CHAPTER ONE

The Basics of Relationship Communication

Life would be so much easier if it came with an instruction manual you could give other people on how to communicate with you in a way that you never feel misunderstood, triggered, or unheard. Many people grow up in families where communication comes in the form of arguing; for some, there is no communicating at all. If you're one of the lucky ones, you may have witnessed your parents' relationship as being healthy, with the ability to communicate about almost anything and repair whenever communication went off the rails.

In a broad view, healthy communication is broken down into two parts: verbal and nonverbal. I always tell the couples I work with, "It's not what you say, but how you say it," and it's the experience of being heard, understood, or criticized that the other person has when they are communicating with you. Are you distracted? Are you making eye contact? If so, what do your eyes say? Are you turned toward your partner? This chapter will review those components to healthy communication and paint a picture of the tools and exercises you'll learn throughout this book.

TWO DIFFERENT
COMMUNICATION STYLES

Kayla and Andrew have been married for about three years. Throughout their dating history, communicating came effortlessly to them. They barely fought and on the off chance that they did, they were easily able to take responsibility and forgive each other, which ended their disagreements quickly.

Both Kayla and Andrew work full-time and have been saving up to buy a house. Kayla has talked frequently about wanting children sooner rather than later. Andrew is concerned about the affordability of having a child, and he tries to steer away from conversations about having children as quickly as possible.

Kayla has become increasingly frustrated by Andrew's avoidance of the topic. Their conversations quickly escalate, and they often end up on separate sides of their tiny apartment. Kayla grew up in a house where conflict was talked out and sometimes there was arguing. Andrew's family kept conflicts private, and he doesn't remember his parents having any deep discussions or arguments in front of him or his siblings.

The couple eventually realized that they both have different conflict styles stemming largely from their respective childhoods. They decided to seek out a counselor for support in learning how to communicate in a way that made both partners feel comfortable, especially around challenging topics like finances and having kids. Now that the couple has learned communication tools, they are able to recognize the effectiveness of taking breaks from conversations, identifying their feelings, and sharing their needs in a way that both of them can better respond to.

What Relationship Communication Means

You and your partner each have different backgrounds and styles of communication that you're used to or easily revert to. In Kayla and Andrew's story, you see that even though they really care about each other, they each came from families that had different styles of communicating. The way in which each of them tried to communicate was based on their individual comfort levels with conflict, and not from the standpoint of building a new and healthy dynamic for themselves as a couple.

Before you can learn to communicate well, you must first understand what you believe to be true about communication, where you learned how to communicate, and why you have the responses to certain topics that end up being hot-button issues between you and your partner. Relationship and communication education that is centered in research-backed approaches will provide structure and clarity for even some of the most challenging topics.

Communication tools that you will learn in this book will give you and your partner the ability to stay calmer in arguments, state your point and feelings without blame, and find the ability to compromise with your partner where both people's core needs are seen and honored. Communication is the backbone to any healthy relationship, and you very well may be doing the best you can with the lessons you have learned. You don't know what you don't know. Having the right tools can create a lasting impact and legacy in your relationship and family for generations to come.

You Don't Have to Be in Conflict to Improve Your Communication

Research conducted by the Gottman Institute reveals that couples who undergo premarital counseling have a 30 percent reduction in divorce rates, due to the higher awareness of their differences and tools they learn to reduce conflict. Regardless of whether or not a couple is experiencing conflict, they can benefit from learning communication tools for the relationship, as well as from developing an understanding of themselves personally and how they relate to others.

Whether you have a healthy relationship where conflict is addressed with curiosity and empathy or a relationship that's mired in conflict you can't seem to get through, this book will give you the tools to navigate it. If you learn how to have conflict and communicate more effectively, and if you're willing to use the tools, you'll be able to talk about anything. That doesn't mean you'll fix everything in your relationship, or that your relationship will be perfect. You'll just have a better way to navigate through the inevitable challenges you'll face as a couple.

It is normal to be afraid of conflict and want to avoid it at all costs. But couples who have conflict are sharing their feelings and needs, and when they do it well, it can benefit the relationship tremendously. For the purposes of this workbook, "conflict" is when two people have completely different viewpoints, experiences, needs, or feelings when they're talking about the same topic. Learning to hear each side without judgment is your first step in building a healthier communication dynamic. Allow your partner to be different from you, hear their perspective without casting aspersions, and seek to deepen your understanding of their perspective before moving on to resolve an issue.

The Benefits of Strengthening Communication in Your Relationship

If you can't communicate with your partner, you can't grow and evolve throughout life together. Most partners believe they are communicating well. Yet, when talking through a conflict, there are unexpressed feelings, blame, and needs that are often masked as criticisms. You and your partner can both benefit from reminders, education, and support to strengthen your relationship.

The benefits of strengthening your communication as a couple include a deeper understanding of yourself and each other, increased intimacy, a more positive outlook on your relationship, the development of shared meaning, and your relationship leaving a legacy. Strengthening your connection means constantly staying curious about your partner and about their intentions, needs, and feelings. Relationships tend to struggle once you start building assumptions instead of asking questions, or when you stop yourself from sharing because you don't feel like your partner is open to hearing your side of the story. Your relationship suffers, sometimes irreparably, as soon as you start believing that in every conflict there is a right side and a wrong side.

Deeper Understanding of Each Other

I can't tell you how many times I've heard "I don't know" as the answer to a question meant to gain clarity about a person's feelings, needs, or experience. In order to communicate with others, slow down and consider first the feelings that are driving your behavior and what you want to get out of having this conversation with your partner. Knowing that and then communicating it effectively to your partner will improve your understanding of yourself and your partner. You'll be given a process for this later in the workbook.

Increased Intimacy

Intimacy is about so much more than sex. It's also about feeling known and seen by your partner in a way that is different from the other relationships in your life. As you dive deeper into your own experience and your partner's, you will begin to develop a deeper and more intimate connection that is different from all the other relationships in your life. This will increase the desire to connect and share yourself in other ways, too. When intimacy in communication is restored, your amount of trust increases tremendously. Trust is what everyone wants in a relationship. In this workbook, you will learn how to develop and *sustain* it.

A More Positive Outlook on Your Relationship

When communication and conflict are productive, you are able to develop more trust and reassure yourself that it's all right to have needs and share feelings with your partner. If communication and conflict are unproductive, there is likely to be a tendency to convince yourself to bottle up emotions, get louder, or avoid conflict altogether. What you perceive about your partner and your communication impacts how you behave in the relationship. Strengthening your communication will shape a more positive narrative that leads to better, more productive conflict.

Shared Meaning and Relationship Legacy

If couples don't learn to move through conflict and talk about difficult things, they will be left with questions and without many answers. What are you building? Where are you going? How are you teaching children in your house to be in a relationship? It is normal to want to know why you're in the relationship.

I want you to walk away from this book with answers that make you excited for the future and clear about the purpose of your relationship. There are many different forms that and reasons why people stay together. Discussing this with your partner will help with clarifying values and how those show up in your experience and decisions.

The Key Signs of Healthy Relationship Communication

Because you picked up this book, it is likely that you want concrete information and tools that help you critically evaluate what and how you're communicating with your partner. There are key signs to look for when assessing how the communication can improve in your relationship. Those signs include practicing radical honesty, practicing acceptance without judgment, listening to understand, and assuming and verbalizing positive intent.

These overarching concepts appear to be simple and straightforward, but the practice of applying them is typically much more difficult. It is common to enter a conflict with your guard up and ready to fight to win your case. Practicing these concepts means going into that conflict with a vulnerability and willingness to be curious, potentially flexible, and open to different ideas.

Many people are taught to view vulnerability as a type of weakness. Brené Brown's research on vulnerability in her book *The Gifts of Imperfection* showcases that courage is synonymous with vulnerability. Vulnerability is all about risking your heart and yourself for a greater good. However, having the depth of connection that partners typically say they want requires slowing down, getting in touch with your emotions and triggers, and developing an understanding of why you think or feel the way you do instead of just reacting. You are able to show greater gentleness and openness with your partner when you extend that same gentleness and openness to yourself.

Radical Honesty

It has been my experience that couples' relationships end due to lies. Lies can come in the form of withholding information or giving details that are completely different from what really happened. Lying is a form of manipulation that many people use knowingly and unknowingly, to protect themselves or their partner's image of them.

Radical honesty starts within you. The hardest part comes after, which is to share that honesty with your partner. Being radically honest means that you respect yourself and your partner enough to be your most authentic and flawed self. Relationships that have the potential for getting healthier or maintaining health can withstand hard truths.

Acceptance without Judgment

What is acceptance? It's the allowance for another person's flawed humanity. Now, that doesn't mean a person can keep making mistakes and you allow it. That is another topic that will be addressed when it comes to boundaries.

When you seek to build an understanding of how your partner's mind works and the experiences that shape their mindsets and assumptions, you can extend more grace and have more intentional conversations about needs and assumptions around each other's actions. If you've built a good map of how your brain and your partner's brain work together, and separately, you can also make quicker attempts to reconnect after an issue or trigger arises.

Listening to Understand, Not to "Win"

You can't really understand what your partner is trying to say or what they need when your mindset is fixated on only your side of the story. This is where the need for curiosity in conflict really comes into play. Instead of talking over your partner, give them direct eye contact, ask questions that can't be answered with a simple yes or no, and provide a summary of what you heard, to ensure that you understand what they are trying to communicate. You don't have to agree with your partner to practice this. It's a better way to engage in conflict, because you can hear better when you feel heard. As a result, you will see fewer triggering experiences in conflict and increased empathy, which leads to reduced intensity in times of conflict.

Assuming and Verbalizing Positive Intent

Whatever you believe about your partner and their intent will determine how you show up in a conflict. The next time you're listening to your partner, ask yourself, "What is the story I'm telling myself about their intentions?" Maybe you believe they don't care or that they're only protecting themselves. If so, ask yourself, "What evidence do I have that this is true?"

Next, consider that your partner has positive intentions and doesn't want to harm you. How might that impact your reaction or ability to ask questions in conflict? Try saying something like "I know you don't want to hurt me, but I can't help but wonder if you could try saying that with more softness." Assuming and verbalizing positive intent will greatly assist to develop and grow your communication as a couple.

Is Your Relationship Communication Healthy?

Without judging each other, use this quiz to talk through where you are alike and where you are different in your communication style. Each of you will take some time to answer either "T" for "True" and "F" for "False" to the following statements. Circle the response that best corresponds to your answer.

Partner A   **Partner B**

T F **1.** When I'm upset with my partner, I need time away to think.   T F

T F **2.** When I'm upset with my partner, I have to talk it through right away.   T F

T F **3.** I believe my partner is curious about my feelings on a daily basis.   T F

T F **4.** I feel curious about my partner's feelings on a daily basis.   T F

T F **5.** My partner and I spend time together every day checking in with each other.   T F

T F **6.** I feel close and connected to my partner.   T F

T F **7.** I feel hopeful and optimistic about our relationship.   T F

T F **8.** My partner and I dream and talk about our future as a couple regularly.   T F

T F **9.** I feel like I can share everything with my partner.   T F

T F **10.** I am afraid of being judged by my partner when I share my thoughts, feelings, and experiences.   T F

continued ▸ ▸

T   F   **11.** I can put aside my own point of view in conflict and   T   F
really listen to my partner's side of things.

T   F   **12.** My partner can put aside their own point of view in   T   F
conflict and really listen to my experience.

T   F   **13.** I assume my partner's intentions in conflict are   T   F
intended to be positive and for the greater good of
our relationship.

T   F   **14.** I share my appreciation of my partner with them daily.   T   F

Assessment Key: This assessment is designed to get a clearer look at what
may be the strengths and growth areas in your relationship. Couples answer
these questions differently, and it may be helpful to share your answers
with your partner for better clarity on each other's perspective as you move
throughout the rest of this book.

Every Relationship Benefits from Improving Communication

Learning to communicate more effectively can feel daunting. You're not alone. Many couples come to my office already exhausted from trying to communicate on their own, and they wonder if there is any hope for them.

This book is meant not to make life more complicated, but to simplify it. When you improve the communication in your relationship, it helps you improve your communication with others in your life, from friendships and children to family members and co-workers.

You may find that there are some parts of this book and tools that you have already mastered. Celebrate that! Other parts of this book will provide eye-opening insight and awareness to key growth areas for you in your relationship. Life is always evolving and changing. When you learn how to communicate, you can move through ever-changing challenges with greater ease.

Research validates that a couple's communication improves dramatically when they spend time being friends. Being your partner's friend includes spending time together, being curious with each other, sharing appreciation, and communicating needs. The demands of life often take you away from those small but meaningful moments. This book will provide structured ways to make sure that you and your partner are prioritizing the relationship in your lives the way that you want to.

KEY TAKEAWAYS

- Every relationship can benefit from learning tools to communicate more effectively. Whether your relationship is newer and communication comes easy, or you've been together for a long time, you can learn to build structure to the way you connect and move through conflict.

- You each have a conflict style and beliefs about what constitutes healthy and unhealthy conflict. You often learn those from caregivers and your peers. Many times, your styles are different from each other, and that creates additional stress and pressure in conflict.

- Strengthening your communication allows you to develop a deeper understanding of yourself and your partner, and to increase the feeling of closeness and intimacy by sharing needs. It also enables you to develop and sustain a more positive outlook on your relationship and life in general, and to open up your mind to the possibilities in your relationship and that future you're building together.

- In order for healthy communication to be sustainable, there must be structure. Life is constantly changing and evolving. It's important to develop time in your schedule to practice checking in, with yourself and with each other, about your feelings, needs, and perspectives on the experiences you have together, as well as their positive and negative impacts on the relationship.

CHAPTER TWO

How Miscommunication Happens in a Relationship

It is common to think that you're communicating your thoughts, feelings, and needs clearly. Unfortunately, by the time couples end up in my office, they often discover that has not been the case. As I mentioned earlier, how you say something can impact the outcome of a conversation more than what you say.

Your communication style is different from your partner's, and for that reason, you need to know the rules of the game when it comes to communicating. You can ensure greater success in communication when you learn to slow down, get to know yourself, and share things when you are not in the heat of the moment. It is less likely that you will communicate effectively when you are upset or feeling hurt by your partner.

In this chapter, you will learn the common causes of miscommunication, discover your communication styles, learn how upbringing shapes how you communicate, and find out how miscommunication can lead to relationship conflict. The sign of a healthy relationship is not the absence of conflict, but a couple's ability to make repair attempts both during and after it. If you're not having conflict, are you really sharing your fullest self with your partner?

TASHA AND ERIN

Tasha grew up in a home where you didn't talk about issues, including those happening in relationships. You put your head down and kept working. If there was a feeling, you stuffed it down deep inside and pretended it didn't exist. That continues to be her strategy for her work life and her relationship with Erin.

Erin grew up lonely and often sought nature as a reprieve. She longed to talk and share her feelings with someone—anyone. Getting married was supposed to be one of the best feelings in the world.

The couple enjoyed an idyllic relationship for more than five years, until they began to face stressors and challenges that eventually made them adversaries instead of partners. With their differences in communication styles and needs, conflicts escalated quickly but never ended with any kind of compromise or closure. They would fight until one couldn't take it anymore. They began isolating themselves from each other, and intimacy went down the drain. If they did communicate, it was usually about household or financial issues. Neither partner felt heard, seen, or connected to each other.

Through counseling, Tasha and Erin began to learn the tools of speaker and listener. Feelings began to be identified and processed through, and needs were shared. The couple found they weren't as afraid of sharing their concerns with each other. They also felt more hopeful about maneuvering through conflict in a respectful way that led to a deeper understanding of themselves and each other, and they became more capable of making compromises along the way.

Understanding Your and Your Partner's Communication Styles

Renowned psychologist John Gottman is best known for his work in studying couples, communication, and what makes love last. Through more than forty years of research, Gottman and his team have identified four main components in couples' dialogue that result in relationship instability and high potential for divorce: criticism, defensiveness, contempt, and stonewalling.

I call criticism the gateway drug. When a conflict discussion begins with a "you" statement, it is inevitably met with defensiveness, and you will go back and forth blaming and defending each other. Next comes contempt, where you start to talk down to your partner or call them names because you don't feel heard by them. In an attempt to self-soothe, one or both partners then go into stonewalling, which can feel like you're talking to a wall. Conversations are avoided, and all you receive from your partner is an uncomfortable chill.

Your relationships with people and what you expect from them largely depend on your caregivers' past ability to see and meet your needs. If you were allowed to have and share your feelings and needs, you are typically more open to your partner's. Conversely, if you had to fend for yourself and feelings or needs weren't discussed, you are more likely to expect that your partners take care of themselves. You need to know what tools you are using to protect yourself, and to practice treating your partner as if they have good intentions and care about your feelings in order to better your communication.

Common Causes of Miscommunication

There are common reasons why couples fail to really hear each other during conflict that make them avoid it altogether. Those usually include not knowing or not sharing the root of the issue, making quick assumptions and judgments, and not clearly understanding each other's wants and needs.

In order to know how you are miscommunicating, you must first begin to know yourself, slow down your responses, do an internal check-in, and communicate from a place of ownership your own feelings and needs. You are personally responsible for how you show up in conflict and acknowledging when you make mistakes.

It's extremely important to take feedback from your partner. You may be trying to share your thoughts calmly and carefully, yet they still feel attacked or misunderstood. This is a hard process because everyone interprets information differently. Your partner may want to hear you, but their interpretation of what you're saying doesn't match your intent.

Avoiding the Root of the Issue

Typically, you rarely fight about what you're actually fighting about. It's never about the dishes not being done or the fact that you haven't had sex in a month. So, you need to slow down and ask yourself, "What am I truly fighting about in this situation?"

Much relationship conflict centers on one or two things that present themselves in different ways. For example, you may be fighting to feel seen, heard, connected to, or prioritized. Identifying and sharing that core need with your partner will help increase empathy, understanding, and clarity for both of you. Tell your partner, "I'm feeling lonely in this relationship because our children and work lives take priority. I really need to build a connection with you by doing a nightly check-in and having a weekly date night." With this approach, you are more likely to see a different, positive response from your partner.

Making Assumptions

It is common to make assumptions based on past behaviors and your fears for the future. If you think you know everything about your partner, you may make quick assumptions regarding their intentions and how they might respond.

The goal is to go into a conflict discussion with an open mind and curiosity for what your partner may be thinking and feeling. Give your partner an opportunity to build trust with you so that they can and want to show up better for you. If you find yourself making an assumption, share it. That can look something like "The story I'm telling myself is that I will have to take care of all the household responsibilities because you're too busy. However, I want to hear what your intentions are about helping around the house and how you feel you can build that in as a priority."

Misunderstanding Wants or Needs

Unfortunately, wants and needs are often talked about only after they haven't been met for a while. Naturally, there can be defensiveness and criticism involved with how you share those wants and needs with your partner. Many people can't even articulate what they want.

Remember, your feelings steer you in the direction of what your needs may be. First, identify the emotion that you are experiencing right now. Maybe you feel lonely in your relationship. Next, identify the emotion you want to feel—perhaps it's an emotion that will help you feel more connected with your partner. Finally, ask yourself, "What would be happening in my relationship right now if I was feeling connected?" This is a great way to identify your wants and needs.

How Miscommunication Leads to Relationship Conflict

Conflict is having completely different emotions or interpretations of the same event. You likely jump into conflict with the idea that there is only one way to look at this event: that it's through your lens, and your partner is wrong. When that happens, you will often go round and round in circles without ever getting anywhere.

Take that same idea into bigger themes of conflict, such as sex and intimacy issues, career or financial struggles, and household or family obligations, and you may already be feeling shut down about dealing with these issues. It's important to come into any bigger conflict knowing that it may never fully go away. The goal is to understand that the same issue may continue to recur throughout your life together and you need to learn how to communicate about it. If both of you have differing perspectives, needs, or expectations, you will have to learn to communicate often about them and be willing to make compromises.

Effective compromise is being able to recognize your core needs around each topic. A core need is something that you cannot give up or it would feel like giving up a piece of yourself. Identify your areas of flexibility around an issue. Areas of flexibility are often things like when or how something happens, or who causes it to happen, and you are willing to have more conversations about this particular strategy. Then you can take a temporary or partial step forward in your areas of flexibility and continue to check back in with each other.

How Your Upbringing Can Impact Your Communication

Regardless of whether you had a positive upbringing experience or a negative one, you learned what to expect in relationships and how you want to show up in them. Those early relationships also taught you what you can or want to expect in your romantic partnerships.

Think about how your parents or guardians used to communicate with each other. Would they fight in front of you, or would they never fight at all? Did their relationship end abruptly, and you had no idea why? Did they have the "perfect relationship" that you aspire to have? Talk over these questions with your partner and note how different your answers may be.

Explore together how some of the same tendencies you watched in your parents' relationship may be manifesting in your own. For example, if your parents never fought in front of you, you may rarely bring up issues with your partner because you believe that isn't what you do. You go to work, come home, and deal with the day-to-day issues, but you never broach your feelings or needs in the relationship. On the other hand, if your parents shared everything with each other, you may believe that's what you want in the relationship with your partner. Use these questions as an opportunity to explore your family differences together and how they may be impacting your expectations.

Sex and Intimacy Issues

Most couples have different sex drives. There is generally one partner who needs emotional and physical closeness outside of just having sex, while the other partner needs sex to feel connected. Neither one is wrong, but what often happens is that you wait for the other person to do what you want them to do before you make any attempts to give them what they need.

Think about how you can each take a step closer toward meeting the other's needs. That may look like asking for cuddles on the couch every night and simultaneously making an effort to create a sexual experience one time over the next week.

Career or Financial Struggles

One of you is a spender while the other is a saver. One wants kids right away, and the other wants to wait until their career and finances reach a certain point. Regardless of how different the two of you are, it's important to remember that both of your needs in this relationship deserve to be seen as valid.

Try to consider what you must have in this area to feel secure, and focus on areas where you can give a little. For example, tell your partner, "I want to spend the next six months saving $3,000" or "Let's go see our doctors to get prepared for pregnancy and make sure all our medical stuff is up to date." Doing this may look like progress for both of you, and the goals are concrete. Each of you will have the opportunity to share your needs with each other and the compromise will come after both partners feel heard and understood.

Household or Familial Obligations

Discussing responsibilities around the house or to family can often be uncomfortable and stressful. The important thing here is that you and your partner focus on making each other feel heard, respected, balanced, and prioritized. This is a very common concern among couples because our needs and expectations can change quickly based on work and family pressures.

Consider sitting down once a week to go over what is coming up in the week ahead, and discuss ways that you can support each other with roles and expectations.

Where Do You and Your Partner Miscommunicate?

This assessment will walk each of you through a list of different approaches to conflict. If an approach applies to you, circle "T" for "True." If it doesn't, circle "F" for "False." As you go through the list, keep in mind that there is no good or bad choice. Without judging each other, use this quiz to talk through your feelings or stories around why or why not conflict is healthy in your relationship.

Partner A			Partner B
T F	**1.** I have to talk through conflict in the moment.		T F
T F	**2.** I need time away from the situation before I can talk about it.		T F
T F	**3.** I think conflict is healthy.		T F
T F	**4.** I think conflict is unhealthy in a relationship.		T F
T F	**5.** I can identify my feelings easily and share those with my partner.		T F
T F	**6.** I think there is no point in sharing feelings with my partner.		T F
T F	**7.** I often feel criticized or judged by my partner in conflict.		T F
T F	**8.** We can share our feelings and needs without conflict escalating most of the time.		T F
T F	**9.** My family talked openly about their feelings and needs.		T F
T F	**10.** My family never talked about their feeling and needs.		T F

Navigating Conflict Is Part of Every Relationship

Conflict provides you with an opportunity to learn about yourself and your partner. It also ensures that you are sharing all of yourself with each other, and when done well, it can keep you from building resentment.

The first step in any conflict is to hear, summarize, and validate the emotions that each partner has before moving into developing a concrete plan for change. Make sure that when you enter into a conflict discussion you are in the right mindset. If you're really upset, you may not be able to communicate effectively, or have the empathy or ability to listen to your partner. Practice some self-soothing strategies like distraction, going outside, deep breathing, or journaling prior to having a hard discussion. The tools in this workbook are designed to be used when you are in a calmer, more controlled state of mind.

Go into every conflict discussion believing it's okay that your partner sees an issue differently. The goal is not for you or your partner to be right, but for both of you to hear and respect each other's differences. That includes even if your partner's interpretation of the "facts" is different.

Every conflict experience is subject to your own interpretation. You hear better when you feel heard. So, listen first, take notes, and share with your partner what you heard them say their experiences are or were. Then switch roles and have your partner do the same for you.

KEY TAKEAWAYS

- You learn your conflict styles from your early relationships and what you witnessed in your families.

- A person's conflict style shouldn't be labeled as "bad" or "good." If the styles differ, then the objective is to create one that ultimately works for both of you.

- The first goal of any conflict discussion is to hear each person's side of the issue without judging it, then be able to summarize what you heard them say using your words.

CHAPTER THREE

Building Your Communication Skills Toolbox

It would be so lovely if communicating with your partner and others was easy. Often, it is more about *how* you say something than *what* you say that can make all the difference. For a conversation to be successful, it's important that both partners get the opportunity to have and share their perspective of the issue. Many couples jump into conflict with the idea that there is only one way to perceive or change the situation, and without even trying to, they dismiss their partner's experience.

In this chapter, you will explore the key parts of healthy, effective communication. These components include building self-awareness, listening with an open mind, incorporating vulnerability, taking ownership of your mistakes, being able to identify and articulate your positively stated needs, and learning how to set healthy boundaries. As you read through this chapter, keep in mind that these principles and tools take time to build. If your relationship has been struggling, you may wonder if you even trust your partner enough to practice these concepts together. Trust takes time and consistency, so not every couple starting out on this journey will begin with that trust. However, with the help of these concepts, both of you will build that trust over time.

MIKE AND ISABEL

Mike was known for making quick, impulsive decisions. He wasn't used to slowing down and asking for help or considering options from anyone else. Isabel found this charming and confident at the beginning of their relationship. After a while, though, she felt left out and bulldozed into decisions that she never signed up for. For a long time, it seemed like their fights went nowhere. Threats were made with no follow-through, and the couple found themselves distancing from each other, piling up a lot of hurt and resentment as they did so. Even talking about where to go for dinner felt like a chore that neither one of them wanted to talk about.

Isabel and Mike knew they still wanted to be together, however. Starting to work through the communication tools they had been hearing about felt scary and sometimes overwhelming. They committed to adopting these tools and letting each other know if they were feeling judged or not listened to in the moment. Letting each other know calmly that the tools weren't being used was a great reminder to get back on track. Over months of consistency, the couple was able to start having more productive conversations and making temporary compromises on hot-button topics.

A Dialogue Takes Two

Communication is a two-way street. Having one partner pull the weight of change will only take a couple so far. It is important that each partner takes the time to invest in the relationship to ensure its success. It is not uncommon for one partner to believe that they work harder in the relationship, or that they feel resentful because they want their partner to actively be a part of making things better.

The goal of this workbook is to give you concrete tools. Even if your partner is not a part of going through this workbook with you, be sure to let them know about the tools you are trying, and explore what you would like their involvement or reaction to be around the use of those tools.

Attempting to use all the tools in this workbook at once can be overwhelming. As you sift through them, start with a tool that makes sense to your relationship dynamic. For some, it can be challenging to start with sharing vulnerably with their partner because the relationship has gone through hard times or they may not know how to be vulnerable. It's often good to start practicing self-awareness first—in order to communicate clearly and without criticism, you must start with yourself. I recommend that couples spend an average of twelve hours a year investing in their relationship through counseling, reading books, or attending conferences to keep tools fresh in mind.

How This Workbook Can Help

This workbook will provide you with clear tools and a foundational understanding of how to communicate effectively even in challenging subjects. Research from the Gottman Institute showcases that, on average, 70 percent of a couple's conflict is perpetual. This means couples are fighting about the same thing over and over again, in different ways, because they are two different people with completely different experiences.

The goal isn't necessarily to rid the relationship of conflict, but to teach you how to maneuver and find compromises to resolve conflict. Keep in mind that you are not really ever fighting about what you're fighting about. You and your partner are usually fighting for something. This workbook will help you examine what you're truly fighting for in this relationship and how to make headway on these gridlocked issues with an open and willing mind.

Vulnerability comes through time and practice, and as you begin to lower your guard with each other, you will become better able to practice taking ownership of your mistakes, identifying your needs, and setting healthy boundaries.

Building Self-Awareness

Self-awareness comes from intentional focus on listening to your own thoughts, learning how patterns in your life developed, and asking for feedback and support from trusted people in your life and/or a counselor. You build self-awareness from a true desire to grow, even when that growth is painful and will require change.

One of the best places to start with self-awareness is recognizing and tracking emotions. Your emotions often dictate your behaviors and reactions. If you can begin to name your emotions, you can also learn how to tame them.

Listening with an Open Mind

Jumping into a conversation with the belief that you aren't the only one who is right is the best way to begin practicing the art of having an open mind. Looking at things purely in black-and-white terms is a form of self-protection used in relationships to avoid getting hurt. Opening your minds to different perspectives, feelings, or experiences creates within you a level of vulnerability, and questioning that helps you grow personally and relationally. Knowing that, please understand that these tools to communication require a level of change that one must prepare themselves for, and have adequate support to work through.

Becoming Comfortable with Vulnerability

"Vulnerability" is the ability to sit or wrestle with new or hard truths that require change, empathy, and leaning into the unknown. It requires that you jump from the mindset of "I'm sure it's this or that" to that of "I don't know what this will mean for me or us, but let's figure it out together." Vulnerability moves you from the safe and self-protective waters of the big gray world of the unknown, which often forces you to challenge a lot of what you've learned and practiced for much of your life.

Owning and Addressing Your Mistakes

You play a role in the dynamic of your intimate relationships. Whether you like it or not, personal responsibility is necessary to growth in your relationship. Putting all the blame on your partner, or waiting for them to change first, won't get you anywhere. When your partner does something that you don't like, are you reacting in a way that keeps the pattern going? What are you allowing that you don't like and how do you need to set better boundaries and expectations?

If you give over responsibility for only your partner to change in the relationship, both of you are missing out on key growth and development areas. Furthermore, your partner will be less likely to make sustainable change and only grow more resentful.

Being Direct about Your Wants and Needs

When you are hurting in a relationship, it is likely you do one of two things: You don't share your needs at all, or your needs come out as criticisms. Behind every "you" statement that you direct at your partner, there is an unmet need underneath it. If you find yourself constantly stewing on or telling your partner what they aren't doing, then slow down and ask yourself, "What do I really need here?"

Share your needs from a positive perspective. Ask for what you want instead of focusing on what you're not getting. Instead of saying "You don't make time for us anymore," try "I want time alone with you in the evenings."

Establishing Healthy Boundaries

Boundaries look like what is okay as opposed to what is not okay about a situation. You can communicate your boundaries if you know what you are willing to accept and what you are not. For example: "I completely understand that you have work to get done in the evenings. However, I need us to carve out time on our calendars for a date on the weekends."

Building boundaries takes time and practice, and it often means disappointing others or feeling guilty for having needs. This will be discussed later in the workbook.

When to Seek Guidance from a Relationship Counselor

It's my personal belief that all couples can benefit from seeing a counselor to identify and talk through issues in their relationship. There are many books on relationships out there that can provide the tools for a healthy connection. If your relationship has suffered from an attachment injury like an affair, addiction, or lying, then getting the help of a counselor is crucial.

Also, consider how confident you feel in your—or your partner's—ability to really be able to listen without defensiveness. You may find while trying the tools that both you and your partner are getting stuck in certain parts, and you end up more upset than you were at the beginning of the conversation. That's when it can help to have a trusted and educated third party like a counselor to help you move through more challenging decisions and conflicts. Childhood or relationship trauma from the past can also make it hard to use foundational tools. In that case, seeing a couple's counselor who is also trauma-informed will be extremely helpful.

You don't know what you don't know about building a healthy relationship. The goal of working with a counselor is to have an assessment done of your relationship to identify the strengths and growth areas that are unique to you as a couple. Having a trusted counselor for when things inevitably hit a rough patch will keep you and your partner from having to navigate issues alone or letting them worsen.

The Benefits of Setting Short- and Long-Term Goals

In order to make any real progress toward the life and love you desire, you have to be clear about what it is you're doing, and how you're going to keep doing it. Your long-term goals reflect where you want your relationship to be in regards to communication and connection. Short-term goals reflect what you're going to do daily, weekly, and/or monthly to obtain your long-term objectives.

It is normal to want lasting change immediately and to forget that change is a process that takes time. What you do every day with intention ultimately gives you the life and love you want versus thinking about it and trying to do it all at one time. Instead, set yourselves up for success, and consider taking one or two small steps at a time. While you're doing that, dream about and plan for what you each want in a lasting and loving relationship, based on what you learn in this book and have gleaned from your life experiences.

Remember: Change Takes Time

Your communication style is likely very different from your partner's. The first step comes from trying to identify what your and your partner's communication style is, then understand where it came from and how it may still protect you during conflicts. You can't make lasting change until you understand your baseline without judgment.

Next, you'll take one or two exercises from this book to practice in your daily lives. You'll agree on one that you believe will help the most in your relationship and how both of you will actively practice it daily. Finally, you'll practice how to check in with each other frequently, to ensure the tools are working or if adjustments have to be made. Though it is true that change takes time, it's not so much about the endpoint as it is the journey of better learning about yourselves and each other that means the most to many couples. You're always evolving and changing, so your relationship has to evolve and change as well.

When you start this journey, don't be surprised that many things you both may have pushed down may come up. Try to remind each other that you can't fix everything at once, but that you are a team in making your communication better over time.

What Are Your Communication Goals?

This assessment provides fill-in-the-blank sentences to process what you want your communication style to look like with your partner and the important issues you'd like to be able to discuss without conflict. After that, you will find several suggested topics for each of you to answer and discuss. Be mindful that you aren't problem solving just yet; you're working toward trying to understand each other and being clear about what each other's hopes and dreams are when it comes to communication in your relationship.

1. I wish my partner listened to me when I talked about . . .

Partner A: _____

_____

Partner B: _____

_____

2. I wish my partner was more comfortable discussing . . .

Partner A: _____

_____

Partner B: _____

_____

3. When I share my feelings and perspectives, I wish my partner practiced more . . .

Partner A: _____

_____

Partner B: _____

_____

4. Share a time in your relationship when you felt truly heard by your partner.

Partner A: _____

_____

Partner B: _____

_____

5. Explore with your partner a current issue you have in the relationship that you want to talk more about and why it is important to you.

Partner A: _____

_____

Partner B: _____

_____

6. What is missing in your current communication style with you partner when you two attempt to talk with each other about your feelings and perspectives?

Partner A: _____

_____

Partner B: _____

_____

KEY TAKEAWAYS

This chapter was all about what building a healthy communication skills toolbox will begin to look like for you and your partner. We explored the main components of healthy communication and leaning into change one step at a time. Highlights to take away from this chapter include:

- A healthy dialogue takes two people who are actively listening with a desire to learn instead of being right.

- Effective communication with your partner takes self-awareness of your communication style, where it came from, and how you may still be seeing a benefit of using the communication style you currently have when talking with your partner.

- Vulnerability is built organically over time as each partner takes ownership of their mistakes, allows for two different perspectives, and begins to identify and share their needs without criticism.

- Dream about the long-term goals of communication in your relationship. Think about what being able to connect and talk about anything with your partner might look and feel like. Then you'll figure out the small, intentional steps you can take every day with your partner to draw closer to that reality.

- Change takes time and practice. Allow for grace as both you and your partner lean in and keep trying.

- Some conflict will never go away because you are different people. Learn how to communicate about these issues and work toward making temporary or partial steps forward that are focused on your areas of flexibility, but that also honor each of your core needs.

PART II

PRACTICING YOUR RELATIONSHIP COMMUNICATION SKILLS

I f communicating were easy, everyone would do it well. The reason there are therapists who specialize in this field is because communicating your needs directly, practicing vulnerability, and leaning into your partner's reality through active listening is extremely challenging. The longer a relationship goes without addressing issues around communication, the more deeply entrenched a couple can become in a pattern that they want to break, don't know how to break, or don't trust their partner enough to practice the changes.

In this section of the workbook, you will focus on tools that will help you create change when it comes to how you communicate with each other. There are two things I want each of you to take with you into this section: desire and belief.

Let's start with desire—desire to work together toward a new dynamic. You must both see what the issues are, see your role in them, and have the desire to collaborate on fixing the issues. Second, you must have belief in yourself and your partner that there is effort, good intention, and the ability to change. Your beliefs heavily shape what you perceive in yourself and others. The process of changing old dynamics in your relationship communication pattern will require the belief that change can happen.

Don't mistake belief for trust. Trust takes time and consistency to build up, and it will come later as you see the changes both inside and outside within yourself and your partner.

Throughout this section, you will concentrate on six key themes to better your communication with each other: building self-awareness, listening to understand, becoming comfortable with vulnerability, owning and addressing your mistakes, being direct about your wants and needs, and, finally, establishing healthy boundaries. It's time to dive in!

CHAPTER FOUR

Building Self-Awareness

This will be one of the most important chapters for you to spend your time in. It has been my experience that many couples who come to therapy struggle independently from each other to identify the feelings that drive them, share their needs from a positive lens, and understand patterns from childhood or trauma that may be impacting them in their relationship. Developing self-awareness allows you to communicate more effectively, timely, and with personal ownership in the way that you express yourself. Without self-awareness or the desire to become self-aware, you are likely to spend much of your life going through the motions, accepting less than what you deserve in a relationship, or becoming frustrated and seeking validation and love in unproductive ways.

The exercises, prompts, and practices in this chapter will help you explore your upbringing, identify the feelings that drive your behaviors, and learn how to pick up on and share your needs in a productive way. You will also be provided affirmations that you can use to ground yourself back to the material you're learning, and the effort you are putting in to implement the necessary changes.

KYLE AND MELISSA

Their relationship had been on the rocks for years, and after several failed attempts at therapy, Kyle and Melissa were at a breaking point. Kyle had betrayed Melissa's trust multiple times when it came to sex and intimacy by talking with other women and not discussing with Melissa what he wanted or needed for sexual stimulation. Melissa felt like she was always angry, needed to be "on" all the time, and had to control everything. Kyle would often withdraw and take the criticism because he believed that he deserved to be punished. They fought with each other during the small amounts of time they shared together. Needless to say, intimacy was something that required a lot of working up to, plus the use of alcohol to calm the nerves.

Neither Kyle nor Melissa often shared their needs, and when they did, it was often through criticizing each other. Neither partner felt like they were showing up as their best selves in the relationship, yet they couldn't find a way out of the cycles they were so deeply caught up in.

Thankfully, they eventually found a new counselor who had extensive background and training in high-conflict couples work and sex therapy to support Melissa and Kyle with the unique challenges their relationship faced. Each partner learned how their upbringings showed up in their expectations of the relationship and their perception of each other's intentions. Over the course of a year, the couple began to create routines of connection and checking in, putting a pause between them when things got heated and sharing their feelings and needs without blame. They were also able to recover from the breaches in trust and begin to rebuild their sex life.

REFLECTION CHECK-IN

These check-in points can help set your intentions and bring awareness to the exercises and practices that might be most helpful for you in this chapter. If you already have a great routine for self-reflection, great. If you don't, fear not, because you will develop one throughout the chapter. The curiosity and grace we extend to ourselves will make us more giving of those same things to our partner.

Review the following reflections and circle the response that applies to you. You will have the following options to choose from: "Often," "Sometimes," and "Never." Once your partner has done the same, discuss your responses with each other.

1. I check in daily with my emotions and I can easily describe what I'm feeling.

Partner A:	Often	Sometimes	Never
Partner B:	Often	Sometimes	Never

2. I am able to identify what I need from my partner.

Partner A:	Often	Sometimes	Never
Partner B:	Often	Sometimes	Never

3. I share my needs with my partner without blaming or criticizing them.

Partner A:	Often	Sometimes	Never
Partner B:	Often	Sometimes	Never

4. When I feel overwhelmed or angry, I know how to calm myself down.

Partner A:	Often	Sometimes	Never
Partner B:	Often	Sometimes	Never

5. I know what experiences, feelings, or needs are triggering to me.

Partner A:	Often	Sometimes	Never
Partner B:	Often	Sometimes	Never

continued ▶▶

6. I often pause before I speak to make myself aware of where my feelings are coming from and what I might need.

Partner A:	Often	Sometimes	Never
Partner B:	Often	Sometimes	Never

7. I have a person outside of my partner that I lean on for support, like a friend or counselor.

Partner A:	Often	Sometimes	Never
Partner B:	Often	Sometimes	Never

Pause for a moment and consider what your core needs are in this relationship. Remember that you're never fighting about what you're fighting about; you're at odds over something else, in different ways, over and over again.

In this relationship, what do you believe you're truly fighting for? Are you fighting to have more of a voice, or to have your partner consider you more of a priority? Take time for each of you to think about and write down your answers. Then share and discuss.

Partner A: ....

....

....

....

Partner B: ....

....

....

....

Practicing Self-Reflection

Gaining a better understanding of yourself requires time for self-reflection and mindfulness. It is important to find an outlet that you enjoy and that allows you the time to think through your thoughts and feelings.

Each of you pick one practice that you can commit to doing this week for five to ten minutes a day. Create a practice that fits your schedule and interests. Consider the following examples as ways to create space for self-reflection.

- If you're driving, instead of listening to music or talking on a phone (hands-free, of course), just take in the silence around you.

- If you like art, put paintbrush to paper or journal your thoughts and feelings.

- Read a book about a topic of interest around personal development.

IDENTIFYING YOUR FEELINGS

Your feelings are the drivers of your experience. If you don't know what emotion you are feeling right now or how to respond to it, you can't have much control over how you behave or react. This is the foundation of communication.

For this exercise, you will see a list of emotions in a grid. In the boxes listed next to each emotion, write down a memory of the last time you felt that emotion in your relationship. An example for "lonely" can look like "I sat on the couch to watch a show with my partner last Thursday. Instead of cuddling up next to me, my partner stayed on their side of the couch."

You will build more on this in the following exercises. Right now, you're getting a chance to identify emotions and where they pop up in your experiences with your partner.

EMOTION	PARTNER A	PARTNER B
Defensive		
Lonely		
Loved		
Misunderstood		
Powerless		
Unheard		

As you begin to reflect on your common emotional experience, which emotion do you believe leads most of your interactions with and perceptions of your partner? When you pick out the common emotions, I want you to think about and write down what having that emotion makes you want to do. For example, "If I often feel lonely in my relationship, it makes me want to consider finding a new partner and leaving behind my current relationship."

Partner A: _____

_____

_____

_____

_____

_____

_____

Partner B: _____

_____

_____

_____

_____

_____

_____

_____

Time to Be Mindful

It is easy to go through the day on autopilot. Setting time aside to be more mindful and in the moment helps you better connect with your feelings and needs and be able to share them with your partner more effectively.

Over the next week, practice noticing what times of the day, or what interactions, you have with your partner that trigger the dominant emotions you listed in the previous prompt. Notice your immediate reactions to the trigger or the feeling you are having. This is a practice of mindfulness that helps you become more aware of how you behave on a frequent basis in regard to this relationship.

You may notice that your personal protective walls go up, and you withdraw or think negatively about the relationship. You may also notice you pick a fight that pushes your partner away even though you want them to become closer with you. Take note so that you can work to make your responses beneficial to your relationship communication.

IDENTIFYING YOUR PARTNER'S FEELINGS

In the process of becoming a good listener, it's important to be curious about or aware of your partner's driving emotion. Oftentimes, you may focus too much on whether you agree with your partner's experience, instead of simply acknowledging their feelings. This is a practice run at becoming aware of your own bias or experience with your partner's emotions.

This exercise includes a list of emotions. In the box next to each emotion, have each partner write down a time you think your partner experienced that emotion in your relationship.

It's okay if you don't know the answers to complete this exercise. This is about learning your assumptions and perceptions about your partner. You will share these assumptions with each other in an upcoming exercise and build on them from there.

EMOTION	PARTNER A	PARTNER B
Defensive		
Lonely		
Loved		
Misunderstood		
Powerless		
Unheard		

It is okay for my partner and me to have different emotions and perceptions around the same event.

Asking Open-Ended Questions

Incorporating open-ended questions into partner communication is important for learning new things about your partner and reducing assumption making. Assumptions keep you locked in patterns of behavior that may no longer suit you and/or your partner, and cause long-term damage to the relationship. The goal of this practice is to slow down assumption making and increase intimacy through awareness and curiosity.

It's important to keep curiosity fresh in the relationship and allow for both of you to change and evolve throughout the course of the relationship. This week, make it a point to think about areas of your partner's life you want to understand or learn more about. Consider how they view their stressful situation at work and why they continue to do the work they do. Maybe wonder out loud with them what they believe the benefit they are getting from maintaining certain relationships. Make it a goal to ask each other an open-ended question one time per day over the next week.

AM I CORRECTLY ASSUMING?

Building upon "Identifying Your Partner's Feelings" (page 49), it's time to share your assumptions with your partner about their experience. This is meant to open up discussion and learn, not to be right. Open your mind to the possibility that you could be wrong about an assumption you made.

Out loud and one at a time, share your assumption of the time you thought your partner felt each of the listed emotions. If your partner says you got it right, circle "Correct." If your partner says you are wrong, circle "Incorrect."

For the ones you got wrong, ask your partner to explain what emotion was driving the experience you listed. Space has been provided for each of you to make notes of each response. This is an opportunity to learn and explore. Try not to get sucked back into the problem at hand; just listen to your partner's experience. If you find you or your partner are getting stuck on the issue, take a break, then return to the exercise and start at the next emotion.

continued ▶ ▶

EMOTION	PARTNER A	PARTNER B
Defensive	Correct/Incorrect	Correct/Incorrect
Lonely	Correct/Incorrect	Correct/Incorrect
Loved	Correct/Incorrect	Correct/Incorrect
Misunderstood	Correct/Incorrect	Correct/Incorrect
Powerless	Correct/Incorrect	Correct/Incorrect
Unheard	Correct/Incorrect	Correct/Incorrect

Spend some time considering how often you move throughout the day making assumptions about your partner and their impact on your reactions. Asking a question before making a statement helps slow down a potentially negative interaction between partners and reduces assumption making.

Think about a question or two that you can use before sharing your thoughts. Write them down in the space provided and review them as needed. For example, "Tell me more about that," or "Can you help me understand what made you feel sad?" Being mindful of incorporating curiosity can completely change the dynamic and interactions you have with each other.

Partner A: _____

_____

_____

_____

_____

_____

Partner B: _____

_____

_____

_____

_____

_____

_____

_____

Creating a Weekly Check-In

A weekly check-in is beneficial for increasing awareness about what is going on in each other's lives, how you can support each other, and creating intimacy and the feeling of being known and cared about by each other.

Pick a day, preferably during what you would consider to be you and your partner's weekend. Put on your calendar a time when you will check in with each other. Your check-in should last about thirty to forty-five minutes.

During your designated check-in time, give each other three compliments. After that, share any positive and negative emotions you felt that related to your relationship over the past week. Then try to share where those emotions came from, without blaming your partner.

When you are listening to your partner, make sure that you maintain openness without passing judgment. Just listen. Then ask each other, "What can I do to make you feel loved in the week ahead?" This can be the start of a routine that allows the two of to check in with each other on emotions and issues related to the relationship, focus on good things, and ultimately become more intentional with showing love for each other in the way each of you asks for it.

FOCUS FOR THE WEEK CHECKLIST

It's all about being intentional. Taking what you're learning in this book and knowing how to incorporate it in your day-to-day lives. Without routines and intentionality, what you learn will only go so far. Take this one week at a time, and take into account the areas of growth you've learned from this chapter.

In the space provided, create a list of commitments that you will make to each other for the week ahead. This exercise is to help both of you collaborate and commit this to practice throughout the entire week. Make a goal to come up with at least five things you learned in this chapter that you will attempt to practice this week.

Example: Have a daily check-in with each other about your day, over dinner and without having the TV on.

Partner A: ....

....

....

....

....

Partner B: ....

....

....

....

....

Set a time one week from now when you will come back to this checklist and review what you were more mindful of. Also note areas that didn't get the time or attention they needed.

continued ▶▶

Many people start this process with a lot of doubt about their desire to make it work or a lack of trust in their partner's desire to follow through; that is completely understandable. Trust is built through time and consistency. The process of building healthier communication will take time, and it will often be imperfect. The goal is to at least try.

Write down times you saw your partner this week trying to use the tools you've both learned so far. What do you think worked or didn't work? What did you appreciate about their efforts? When sharing these details with your partner, remember to keep the tone as positive as possible. This isn't about telling them what they did wrong; it's about helping encourage them to keep trying.

Partner A: _____

_____

_____

_____

_____

_____

Partner B: _____

_____

_____

_____

_____

_____

Thought Stopping

Focusing on gratitude and things you see yourself and your partner doing well is key to reducing conflict and criticism. You respond better when you feel seen for the things you do well.

Create an environment in your home in which you tell each other good and positive things you see in each other. If you find that you are being overcritical of yourself or your partner, incorporate this practice. Stop the negative thought as soon as you notice it, then choose one thing you have seen yourself or your partner do that has been positive. It can be small and unrelated to the issues that caused the negative feeling or thought in the first place.

Example:

Negative critique: My partner is always making jokes at bad times.

Positive opposite: My partner uses humor to connect when they are uncomfortable or don't know what else to say.

KEY TAKEAWAYS

- Emotions are usually the drivers of your reactions. If you can identify the emotion that you are feeling, you can often control and communicate your reactions in more effective ways.

- Making assumptions about your partner's feelings, intentions, or experiences will shut off curiosity and often cause defensiveness or the feeling of not being seen.

- Ask a lot of questions and make sure they are open-ended. Open-ended questions are questions that cannot be answered with a simple yes or no.

- If your relationship has had its share of ups and downs in the communication department, you may not start these exercises with a lot of hope and trust. That's okay. Trust is built through consistency and time.

- Make time for checking in with each other weekly about the good things that happened in your relationship this past week. Identify areas of growth to ensure that you and your partner are not holding back or internalizing anything, which often leads to resentment.

- When you notice a "negative" feeling or experience with your partner, take a moment to stop and reflect on something they did well that week. It can be small, but redirecting your thoughts can go a long way in reducing defensiveness and withholding feelings from each other.

- Get to know your own feelings. This takes time, but it is necessary to spend time reflecting. In order to tame a feeling, you have to be able to name it.

CHAPTER FIVE

Listening to Understand

In this chapter, you're going to learn what it means to truly understand your partner. The good news is that you don't necessarily have to be born a good listener. You can develop great listening skills, though it takes a lot of practice. The exercises, prompts, and practices in this chapter will center on identifying and building the qualities of a great listener. Those qualities include: learning to suspend your own judgment; building nonverbal communication; being open and curious; and developing the ability to summarize, empathize, and validate your partner's experience of an issue or event.

As a listener, you will discover that it's not your time to share your thoughts about your partner's experience, but learn to develop a mental map of how your partner got from A to Z in their recollection and emotions related to the issue. A key concept to keep in mind when developing listening skills is that there is more than one way to view an issue or event, and each partner's viewpoints are valid. A partner's experience is valid because it is how they viewed and felt about the issue. If you fight over the "facts," you end up invalidating your partner, and trust in the relationship begins to break down.

CASEY AND TARA

Casey and Tara have been together for almost ten years, and they have one child together. Casey constantly worries about money and having the ability to provide for the family. In an effort to reduce their anxiety, they drink a little every night. Tara believes her partner's anxiety is ruining their marriage, and she often criticizes them for their weight, mood, and lack of desire to better themselves. Casey feels like their partner doesn't even like them anymore.

The couple's fights would revolve around the same things over and over again. Both would end up exhausted, hurt, and avoidant of each other. Eventually, they were like two ships passing in the night, just trying not to collide with each other.

Through reading, listening to podcasts, and going to therapy, Casey and Tara began to learn that both of them were fighting *for* something and not *about* something. Casey was fighting for affection and stability. Tara was fighting for connection. When they started talking about the things they really wanted instead of the things they weren't getting, they were able to better support each other and make progress in their communication. Their arguments turned into dialogue, and they became accepting of each other's needs instead of feeling like their needs were a threat to the other person.

When your needs feel like the opposite of what your partner's are, they can be seen as threats—"I can't get *my* needs met until *yours* are." Moving forward one step at a time toward each person's needs helps reduce resentment and hopelessness.

WHAT ARE THE QUALITIES OF A GOOD LISTENER?

It's time to do a quick check-in about what you and your partner perceive to be the aspects of a good listener.

In this multiple-choice quiz, pick the answer to each question that resonates the most with how you show up as a listener in your relationship.

1. When my partner shares their perspective, I believe . . .

   a. there are "facts" that are black and white in every situation.

   b. my partner has a different side of the story and that's okay.

   c. my partner is always attacking me.

   Partner A: _____ **Partner B:** _____

2. During conflict, I . . .

   a. tend to interrupt my partner to tell them whether what they're saying is right or wrong.

   b. can stay quiet.

   c. ask open-ended questions with genuine curiosity.

   Partner A: _____ **Partner B:** _____

3. Empathy in conflict sounds like this:

   a. "I'm sorry you feel that way, but . . ."

   b. "I can tell this is really hurting you."

   c. "What do you need?"

   Partner A: _____ **Partner B:** _____

Take some time to talk your answers over with your partner. How are the differences in how you answered these questions reflected in how you show up as listeners when you are in conflict?

continued ▶▶

After reviewing the multiple-choice quiz from the previous exercise, do you find that you practice all the qualities of a good listener? If you're not sure or think it's difficult for you to do so, examine why that might be the case. For example, you may really want to listen, but you often feel attacked by your partner's perspective or feelings. Might there be a way to give your partner feedback about how to share their feelings in a softer way? Share this feedback with your partner outside of a conflict discussion to teach each other how to interact in a way that opens up conversation instead of shutting it down.

If you have a tendency to react with defensiveness toward your partner, it can escalate the issue. A great tip to use when in conflict is to say, "I'm going to make a repair attempt here. Can you please try saying that without making blame statements?"

Partner A:

Partner B:

Starting with the Nonverbals

Nonverbal communication is just as important as what you say. Think of your nonverbal language as communicating how open, soft, and present you are for the conversation.

The next time your partner shares that they have something they want to talk about, agree on a mutual time to discuss. When that time comes, put away any electronic devices, have the kids in bed or the dog playing in the backyard. Turn your body to face your partner, give direct eye contact, soften your gaze, and loosen your jaw. Most important, uncross your arms and appear open and relaxed.

This practice is more for your awareness of your body language and what you want to communicate to your partner without saying anything. Once you get situated with your nonverbals, take it a step further. Ask your partner to give you feedback on what they sense from you. In other words, be curious about what they think you're communicating through your openness and willingness to check in.

LEARNING TO TAKE NOTES

In this exercise, you will both practice taking notes about what your partner is saying. As the listener in this exercise, you will not be sharing feedback. Your only job is to write down what you're hearing about your partner's emotions, their perspective on the issue you two have agreed to discuss, and what they may need to make things better next time or to put closure to this incident or issue.

1. Identify who will be the listener for the first part of the exercise. Make sure the listener has something to write on and write with.

2. Decide on a topic to discuss.

3. Ask the speaker to share their feelings first, then share their perception of the issues, and finally their needs.

4. When your partner has completed discussing their viewpoint/emotions/ perspective, and you've completed documenting from your listening perspective, switch roles (remaining on the same topic, or choosing a new one).

When your partner is done sharing, read back what you've heard them say. Start by saying, "I heard you say that you feel [insert emotions stated], this was your experience [their "facts" or perspective], and you need [the needs they expressed]." Ask them if you heard them correctly or if they have anything else they'd like to share or have acknowledged.

Partner A   **Partner B**

Taking what you heard from your partner, what did you learn about their feelings and experience? This isn't something you necessarily need to share with each other. It's an opportunity to observe whether your listening skills deepened your understanding of how your partner perceives things, and, based on what they perceive, how their emotions change or evolve.

Consider a time when you may have made assumptions about your partner's experience in a previous issue, similar to the one that's currently happening, that didn't match their intentions or true feelings and experience. Write about it in the space below, as well as what you think you learned about your partner during the experience.

Partner A: _____

_____

_____

_____

_____

_____

_____

Partner B: _____

_____

_____

_____

_____

_____

_____

Setting Up a Notebook for Continued Learning

Relationships grow cold when you stop learning about each other. You can begin building assumptions, and it grows more difficult to let your partner change over time.

Get a journal or set up an app on your phone that is just for taking notes during conversations with your partner. This is not where you keep a list of their mistakes. This notebook will be where you write your partner's emotions, perspective, and needs. It is your opportunity to practice what you're learning in this workbook long after you're finished reading it.

As long as a couple knows how to communicate, they can learn to communicate about anything. Hearing it once or practicing these tools infrequently will not get you the results you want. It takes daily practice, intention, and focused learning throughout your entire relationship. Assumptions keep us locked in cycles we often struggle to get out of. This notebook will be your reminder to stay curious and always keep learning about your partner.

PRACTICE ASKING SPECIFIC QUESTIONS

Many partners don't know what questions to ask each other when it comes to conflict. This exercise provides you with a list of questions that you can ask during any conflict that will help both of you process feelings and experiences that shape the stories running beneath the surface of your conflict.

Choose a topic that you have often discussed but can't seem to make any headway on. Each of you will practice being the speaker and taking notes. Remember, as the listener, you are putting aside your own perspective, and you are being open-minded, genuinely curious, and attentive with your nonverbals. This will not be an active dialogue, so remember to ask the questions, then stay quiet and listen to how your partner answers. Then switch roles.

1. Tell me why this issue is so important to you.

Partner A: ....

....

....

Partner B: ....

....

....

2. What would be your ideal outcome in this situation?

Partner A: ....

....

....

Partner B: ....

....

....

continued ▸ ▸

PRACTICE ASKING SPECIFIC QUESTIONS continued

3. What specific steps can I take to help you feel supported with handling this issue?

Partner A: ....

....

....

Partner B: ....

....

....

4. Is there a fear or worst-case scenario for you if nothing with this issue changes?

Partner A: ....

....

....

Partner B: ....

....

....

We are a team working together to create a better experience for ourselves when we communicate about difficult things.

Daily Check-Ins

What you practice every day prepares you for when conflict inevitably arises. In this daily practice, you and your partner will each focus on being a listener to each other's experience of a *non-relationship* issue. It could be something stressful your partner is going through with their work or a project they're excited about.

Set about five minutes each to assume the role of listener and speaker. The listener is not there to fix issues, but to encourage the sharing of emotions and let their partner know that they are here to support. Remember, don't play devil's advocate, or try to offer advice unless your partner specifically asks for it. Begin by identifying who is taking which role first. Next, you'll set the timer for five minutes. As the speaker, you are only sharing what is causing you stress *outside* of a relationship issue. This practice gives you an opportunity to get to know each other's inner world on a daily basis, which will increase empathy and understanding over the long haul.

EXPERIENCE TRACKER

Experience matters, and tracking experience helps build and grow your communication in relationship. You and your partner have a lot going on, and even if you care and have the intention to ask about things that are going on in our partner's world, you can easily forget. This exercise will help you remember what to ask about and show you care.

Over the next week, as you practice daily check-ins, use the following chart to track your partner's emotions and what those emotions center on (e.g., work-related events or upcoming projects). For example, if your partner says they're nervous about a huge deadline coming up on Thursday, the hope would be that you'll remember to ask them about how things went afterward.

This exercise may feel forced or too formal. That's okay. However, until something becomes second nature to you, it has to be practiced. Also, using this exercise regularly will instill a sense of trust and progress in the relationship: that you're invested in what each other's day-to-day experience is like, and that you're remembering what your partner is sharing with you.

Partner A *(These are filled out by Partner B)*

PARTNER'S EMOTIONS	STRESSORS/ EXCITING THINGS FOR PARTNER	WHEN TO FOLLOW UP
Worried	Interview with new company	Thursday

continued ▸ ▸

EXPERIENCE TRACKER continued

Partner B *(These are filled out by Partner A)*

PARTNER'S EMOTIONS	STRESSORS/ EXCITING THINGS FOR PARTNER	WHEN TO FOLLOW UP
Worried	Interview with new company	Thursday

Now that you have practiced the Experience Tracker for a few days, think about how you can make this process feel more natural or a better fit for your style. For example, some partners might share that they struggle to find a consistent time each day to practice this exercise and need to adjust when they can do it, like dinnertime or just before bedtime.

In the space provided, list ways in which you can improve the Experience Tracker or make it feel more natural. Once you're both done, share your notes with each other. You may find that you have similar ideas, or you each bring a different perspective to the conversation. There are no wrong answers.

Partner A: _____

_____

_____

_____

_____

_____

_____

Partner B: _____

_____

_____

_____

_____

_____

_____

_____

Practicing Empathy Statements

Sometimes, attempting to be empathetic can come across as being sympathetic or somewhat dismissive. Empathy is when you can put yourself in your partner's experience and allow yourself to tap into the emotions that they're experiencing. It's not just the words you use that communicate empathy; your facial expressions and other nonverbal signals also play a role.

During the coming week, commit to using the provided empathy statements and practices with your partner. Be intentional, because a little empathy goes a long way in defusing arguments and feeling known and seen by your partner.

Empathy statements to use this week:

1. "I know it hurts you when . . ."

2. "No wonder you're upset."

3. "It would be great if you didn't have to worry about this anymore."

4. "I would have also been disappointed by that."

Empathy practices to use this week:

1. Put down your phone (or another electronic device).

2. Turn your whole body toward your partner when they're speaking.

3. Make direct eye contact.

4. Take your partner's hand and rub it with your fingers while they share their feelings.

EMPATHY IS . . . (TRUE/FALSE)

You may want to feel empathy but struggle to really practice it. Couples who have been in conflict for a long time have difficulty refining the ability when they feel really hurt by their partner. Practicing every day when the two of you are not in conflict will help you access empathy when you need it most.

This exercise provides you with a few statements about empathy. Talk with your partner as you go through each statement and determine your own answers, by circling either "True" or "False." Make it a constructive discussion where you can practice asking questions to understand your partner's point of view about each statement.

1. Empathy is being able to identify the emotion your partner is feeling.

   Partner A: True   False

   Partner B: True   False

2. Empathy is saying, "I'm sorry you feel that way" or "I don't want you to feel that way."

   Partner A: True   False

   Partner B: True   False

3. Empathy is acknowledging the emotion your partner shares without judging it or wishing it away.

   Partner A: True   False

   Partner B: True   False

4. Empathy is as much about how I act and what I do as what I do or do not say.

   Partner A: True   False

   Partner B: True   False

continued ▸ ▸

5. Empathy is allowing myself to feel the emotion my partner
is experiencing.

Partner A: True   False

Partner B: True   False

6. Empathy is always agreeing with my partner.

Partner A: True   False

Partner B: True   False

In your attempts to practice empathy, you may get in your partner's head instead of in their heart. Empathy comes from the heart and expresses "I'm in this with you" or "I can feel the emotion that you're feeling right now." This can come from the way you look at your partner and also how you communicate it with your words.

Use the space provided to help you examine your relationship with empathy. Write down where (or if) you believe you learned it, who taught it to you, and what you think about it now. You can then share your answers with your partner, or meditate on what you've written in your alone time.

Partner A: _____

_____

_____

_____

Partner B: _____

_____

_____

_____

Accepting Influence

Accepting influence means that you go into every discussion accepting that there are multiple ways to experience an event or issue.

Before you and your partner move to make changes or decide on an issue, you both want to feel heard. However, because there is often a tendency to focus more on where you differ instead of where you are alike, it can be all too easy to go round and round and get nowhere.

Make sure that both of you have an opportunity to be both the speaker and the listener. After each of you practice listening, taking notes, summarizing, and communicating empathy, make a decision about how to take one step forward with this issue based on what you learned from each other that you agree on. For example, if you two are talking about whether or not to buy a new or used car, in taking turns as both speaker and listener you may have seen that both of you want to gather more information from the dealer. The practice then would be to schedule a time to meet with the dealer to ask more questions before making a decision on a vehicle.

KEY TAKEAWAYS

- The qualities of a great listener include suspending judgment, giving direct eye contact and open body language, asking open-ended questions to show curiosity, taking notes and summarizing your partner's experience using their words, providing empathy, and being able to self-regulate during conversations.

- Empathy means placing yourself in your partner's emotions and experiencing those feelings with them.

- You do not have to agree with your partner to practice having empathy with their emotional experience.

- What you practice every day when it comes to listening and expressing empathy will help you access those tools during conflict.

- There are two sides to every story and experience. Both sides are valid and deserve to be acknowledged.

- When you feel heard, you hear better.

CHAPTER SIX

Becoming Comfortable with Vulnerability

The experience of being known by someone else—or even by yourself—requires bringing your walls down. It means that you have to be willing to expose those parts of yourself that make you uncomfortable. It means risking being hurt and sometimes it means taking the risk of truly being loved.

Vulnerability means that you see others and you let them see you. Your guard is down, and you are willing to keep learning, leaning in, and growing together. You can't force vulnerability with a partner. It is something that grows naturally out of practice, and there's willingness to keep trying and refine self-awareness in front of each other. Many people will ask their partners to be vulnerable when the environment and communication dynamic doesn't bring with them the safety to do so. In this chapter, you will find prompts for self-exploration, exercises to critically evaluate your deepest self, and practices you can do with each other to increase the chances of vulnerability.

MARISOL AND JORDAN

The affairs started several years ago. Marisol tried to deny what she had been seeing. There was a lot of fear of being rejected and abandoned by Jordan. Her father had left her years before. She could never understand what was wrong with her, or why the people in her life never felt like she was good enough. She kept her thoughts and feelings to herself, never really sharing herself with anyone and letting them treat her whatever way they wanted as long as they didn't leave.

Jordan felt like he never really knew his partner. He often felt the sting of rejection whenever he tried to reach out to her. So, he began having affairs to get attention and have his physical needs met. He knew it was wrong and that much of what was happening in his relationship was a result of his own insecurities.

Marisol and Jordan knew that they wanted to be together and not allow others into their relationship. They knew that they had to start talking, set boundaries, and make significant changes to their relationship. Although it was extremely challenging, the more they began to share what was really going on, and the fears they had been keeping from each other, the more love and acceptance they experienced from each other.

WHAT ARE YOU MOST AFRAID OF?

Your beliefs about your partner and their intentions are often the things that drive how you show up in your life and relationship.

As you go through this exercise, take your time to really evaluate what you believe to be true in your relationship with your partner. Each of you is provided a place to circle whether you believe each statement to be "True" or "False." After each of you takes time to answer, it's important to stay curious about your partner's reactions instead of getting defensive. You can't change your beliefs unless you know what they are. This exercise can help you evaluate if there are underlying beliefs that may be keeping your guard up with each other, thereby reducing vulnerability.

1. I believe that my partner loves and accepts me.

Partner A: True   False

Partner B: True   False

2. I believe that my partner would prefer to be with someone else.

Partner A: True   False

Partner B: True   False

3. I used to feel safe and accepted in my relationship, but now I don't anymore.

Partner A: True   False

Partner B: True   False

4. Whenever I share what is going on in my life, my partner always tries to fix me.

Partner A: True   False

Partner B: True   False

continued ►►

5. I feel trusted and good enough for my partner, even if I make mistakes in our relationship.

Partner A: True   False

Partner B: True   False

6. All I do is make mistakes in this relationship.

Partner A: True   False

Partner B: True   False

So many people just want to feel happy, loved, connected, and seen by their partner and in their day-to-day lives. However, not many people can define what those words really mean for them, or believe that they can have them. Sometimes your most desired emotions become the most vulnerable things to ask for and to eventually feel. The reason for that is when you do feel them, you may wonder how long the feelings will last, or if they will be taken from you.

In this space, process and write down what feeling you're looking to have, what it means to you, and if you fear it coming or going.

Partner A: _____

_____

_____

_____

Partner B: _____

_____

_____

_____

Noticing Vulnerable Emotions and Your Reactions to Them

Now that each of you has decided the feelings you're looking for and defined them in the previous prompt, start looking out for those emotions to present themselves in your everyday lives. For example, maybe you defined that happiness means to be fully present in a moment and really share a part of yourself or your life story to someone. You get to be in complete control of being able to accomplish that.

This week, work to embody the definition of the feeling you defined. After you make that attempt, check in with yourself about how you really felt after that—did it give you the feeling that you hoped for and desired? If not, what were your physical and emotional reactions to the definition you gave it?

Afterward, discuss with your partner how connected and hopeful you are about being able to put into practice and feel what it is really like to be happy.

SELF-ACCEPTANCE

Self-acceptance is knowing who you are, what you want, what you like and don't like, and not judging yourself.

In this exercise, each of you will respond to a series of questions or statements. After that, practice some love and gentleness with yourself for who you are and what naturally comes to you.

1. Share one thing about your body that you love.

Partner A: ....

Partner B: ....

2. Are you all right with addressing an issue, or do you prefer to avoid confrontation?

Partner A: ....

Partner B: ....

3. What do sex and intimacy mean to you?

Partner A: ....

Partner B: ....

4. I have the most fun doing this:

Partner A: ....

Partner B: ....

5. I feel the most vulnerable and scared when I'm doing this:

Partner A: ....

Partner B: ....

6. If I could do anything I wanted to for a day, I would:

Partner A: ....

Partner B: ....

Think about how each of you practices acknowledging aspects of yourself–
what you like, and what you don't like doing on a daily basis. Do you believe that
you often reject things about yourself daily and seek to please others? Or do
you find that you have really good boundaries and schedule your day around
what makes you light up? Remember, the goal here is not to judge yourself, but
to *be aware* of yourself.

Write down your thoughts, then share your answers with your partner
afterward to practice opening up with each other about how each of you feels
about yourself.

Partner A:

_____

_____

_____

_____

_____

_____

Partner B:

_____

_____

_____

_____

_____

_____

_____

Daily Practice

A daily practice of checking in with each other showcases prioritizing the relationship. Life often gets busy, and the first thing to go is likely to be communication with your partner. Making a daily practice of checking in will increase empathy and understanding of each other.

Think about the answers you provided in the Self-Acceptance exercise (page 86). Pick one of your answers to focus on over this next week. For example, you can choose an activity that you have the most fun doing and incorporate it into your daily life. You can even choose something that makes you feel more intimate and sexual with your partner, and determine how you can be intentional about doing that this week.

Consider beginning with a small thing that you can do for the next seven days that won't be overwhelming. Consider it your focus point to keep in the front of your mind as you go throughout each day. At the end of the week, share with your partner what you practiced daily and how you feel now that the week is over.

BE CURIOUS ABOUT YOUR PARTNER

Curiosity reduces assumption making and increases your ability to connect and see each other in new ways. This will keep the relationship fresh and potentially reduce conflict significantly.

Ask your partner the following questions and write down their answers. Do your best not to make any judgments about your partner, and don't try to answer the questions for them or assume that you already know their answers.

Go into the exercise with an open mind and a willingness to learn from your partner. Take turns asking each question and writing down answers. You may find that your interpretation of what your partner says is different from their original intention. Writing down each person's answers helps both of you discuss if your intentions and interpretations match.

1. What would be the perfect gift for you at our next special occasion (e.g., anniversary, birthday)?

Partner A: ....

....

....

Partner B: ....

....

....

2. If you could go anywhere alone with me, where would you go and what would we do there?

Partner A: ....

....

....

Partner B: ....

....

....

continued ▶ ▶

3. What is one thing that scares you most about the future?

Partner A:

Partner B:

4. What stresses you out most in your life right now?

Partner A:

Partner B:

5. When do you feel most intimate and close to me?

Partner A:

Partner B:

Intentional Curiosity

In order to keep growing as a couple, it's important that you learn to place a pause point between the information you take in and your reaction to it.

The next time your partner shares something with you this week, ask them an open-ended question. (An open-ended question cannot be answered with a simple yes or no.) For example, if your partner is sharing that they have a lot of work to do this week and that they're really stressed about it, you can ask something like "What tools or structure have you come up with to manage this?"

Curiosity plays a big role in your perception of whether your partner is actually interested in you, in what you think, and in what you're going through. It also decreases assumption making and supports a couple in building emotional intimacy. Slow down the process of jumping in with advice and take a second to think about a question that would help your partner better process what they're going through with you. Examples of open-ended questions include "Tell me more about that" or "I'm wondering what you think about . . ."

*I accept and welcome the fact that my partner and
I are different from each other.*

IDENTIFYING WHAT YOU'VE LEARNED

Because you've been practicing curiosity with yourself and with your partner, set aside time to write down what you've learned so far this week.

On the lines provided, write three things that you've learned about yourself and three things that you've learned about your partner over the past seven days.

Example:

Something that I've learned about myself this week:
"I need to have five minutes to shower after work before talking about my day."

Something that I've learned about my partner this week:
"My partner has a big work project coming up and needs extra time on the weekends to work on it."

If you're starting this exercise not knowing anything you've learned, then you can return to this exercise in a week, after practicing awareness toward yourself and your partner. And remember, these don't necessarily have to be big things you've learned–it can be whatever you've noticed about feelings, reactions, needs, or upcoming/impending stressors.

Partner A

Three things I've learned about myself this week:

1. ....

2. ....

3. ....

Three things I've learned about my partner this week:

1. ....

2. ....

3. ....

Three things I've learned about myself this week:

1. ....

2. ....

3. ....

Three things I've learned about my partner this week:

1. ....

2. ....

3. ....

Take some time in the following lines to process how you see having either a positive or negative impact on your relationship. Think about what you have enjoyed about getting to know each other more, as well as what you'd like to know more about when it comes to yourself and your partner. Discuss your answers together to identify what you may have appreciated learning about your partner, and encourage more awareness about what you want to learn about them in future.

Partner A: ....

....

....

Partner B: ....

....

....

Daily Acknowledgment of Acceptance

It is common to hear things like "I'm sorry you feel that way," "I don't want you to feel that way," or "Think of it like this . . ." The goal of this practice is to get into the habit of acknowledging that you or your partner feel the way you feel.

This week, make it a point to say out loud, both to yourself and to your partner, "I understand you feel or see things that way, and that's okay." If you're up for it, you can go even a bit further and state, "I accept that this is what you need, what you feel, or what you perceive." Acknowledging acceptance can help bring down the defensive walls between you and increase the desire to share more of yourself with each other. It is normal to experience hard emotions and events. You need a safe place to process emotions and experiences associated with hard times. The hope is that as partners you can process all the ups and downs of life together. Feeling heard often goes a long way in a person's ability to motivate themselves to heal.

WRITE A LOVE LETTER

When you first began dating, did you and your partner write love letters to each other? The act of writing love letters is a very personal and intimate exercise.

This week, you will write your partner a letter of love and acceptance for all that you know them to be and for how they show up in life and in their relationship with you. Think about and share the aspects of what you're learning and what you love about them.

When you are done writing your letters, read them to each other. You can tell them what makes you want to work so hard to make this relationship loving and lasting. You can talk about all the things you'd like to learn more about them. Don't rush through this exercise; you can take a couple of days if you need to. You can use the pages made here for you, or you can write it somewhere other than in this book.

Partner A

What I love about you . . .

Partner B

What I love about you . . .

continued ▸ ▸

As you've been spending time evaluating what you know about yourself and your partner, think about areas or gaps in your self-awareness and your awareness of your partner, and what you would like to learn to do better. Are there books, classes, or activities you'd like to experience together or on your own? What are your next steps in building a lifestyle of self and relationship awareness and development?

Collaborate with your partner on making a wish list, and write down the new things that you'd both like to try learning. After that, list the steps that you believe will help make those things a reality. Sitting down and creating a plan together will help you feel more connected and like you're working together to build a future that is meaningful for both of you.

What We'd Like to Try

_____

_____

_____

_____

_____

_____

Making It Happen . . . Next Steps

1. _____

2. _____

3. _____

4. _____

5. _____

6. _____

Stating "We" vs. "I"

Part of being a couple is shouldering whatever this world throws at you, together. You shouldn't feel alone or like you have to do everything yourself when you're in a partnership with someone. In addition to sharing yourself with each other, vulnerability is about providing support to each other.

Think about your individual issues or relationship issues as something you work through together. "We will get through this together," "How can I best support you in this?" and "What do you need?" all communicate a desire to work together to tackle life's challenges. The next time a stressor comes up for your partner, try to avoid saying things such as "What are you going to do?" Instead, address that the problem is a "we" issue that "we" will deal with together. If your partner hears you supporting them, it builds on your communication with each other. It may also encourage your partner to adapt that behavior and support you when you need it.

KEY TAKEAWAYS

In this chapter, you explored what vulnerability is, its barriers in relationships, and how to practice it on a daily basis. Vulnerability isn't something that you can force, but it's vital that you create the environment in your life and interactions that foster it.

- The feelings you most want to have—happiness, connectedness, or being seen and known by your partner—are often the experiences that are scariest. You may not know how to define them, or you may worry that as soon as you experience them, they will be taken away.

- Vulnerability requires self-awareness and self-acceptance. You need to create time and space to learn about yourself so you can share what you learn with your partner.

- Your vulnerability can only grow when there is a curiosity to learn new things instead of relying on old assumptions that keep walls up between you and your partner.

- When it comes to self-awareness, self-acceptance, and relationship development, think about the areas in your relationship that each of you want to be more intentional about practicing, and how you plan to incorporate those tools into your day-to-day life.

CHAPTER SEVEN

Owning and Addressing Your Mistakes

In life, it is easier to focus on self-protection and pointing the finger. Owning and addressing your mistakes is about concentrating more on how your partner feels and not so much on your intent.

Throughout this chapter, you will focus on applying self-reflection strategies, practicing mindfulness and awareness of how your actions impact others, managing your own fears of rejection or hurt that keep you from having productive conversations, and learning how and when to ask for help and feedback. It's important to note that you play a role in the dynamic between you and your partner. If you focus only on your partner's wrongdoing and not on your reactions and behaviors, you most likely won't make it very far in conflict. If you don't like how something is going, you are just as responsible for changing it as your partner is.

TIFFANY AND YASMIN

The relationship started out picture perfect. The connection Tiffany and Yasmin had was instant, and both of them were very intuitive about each other's needs. It was after they moved in together that the cracks of their past relationship issues started to show. Instead of communicating about everything like they used to, they began to withhold issues from each other, which started building resentment. Whenever fights happened, they would be explosive, and they often included threats and accusations that seemed out of proportion to the actual issue they were talking about.

It became clear that something needed to change, or Tiffany and Yasmin wouldn't make it. There was a lot of good in their relationship, and the couple didn't want things to end. They both had to take stock of the triggers and beliefs they developed from past relationships and decide how they wanted to show up differently in this relationship. They began taking ownership of their feelings, sharing their perceptions without blame, and learning to walk away from conversations with clear plans for change and how to make a situation like the one they were dealing with go differently the next time.

Identifying your feelings is important for reducing the intensity of the emotional experience and for helping your partner connect more deeply with you.

1. Focus on the most recent conflict you and your partner had and agree to talk about it. It should be a conflict that you aren't emotionally caught up in, but is an issue that needs to be addressed.

2. Review the provided list of emotions and take turns circling the emotions that were present for you during the issue you chose. If it helps, use different colored pens or highlighters to keep track of whose emotions are whose.

3. Share your emotions out loud with each other, without really explaining them. This chapter will walk you through the entire process.

Sad	Unloved	Abandoned	Unattractive
Misunderstood	Criticized	Exhausted	Not listened to
Powerless	Overwhelmed	My feelings got hurt	Unappreciated
I didn't have a voice	Ashamed	Lonely	Shocked
Mad	Guilty	Opinions didn't matter	Like leaving

continued ▶ ▶

Use this as a time of personal reflection and not something to discuss out loud with your partner. Each of you went through the list of emotions for the conflict you chose to dissect throughout this chapter. What was, or what still is, your initial reaction to your partner's feelings? What does it bring up for you emotionally? Does it make you want to defend yourself, or does it leave you feeling really confused?

Use the space provided to write down the reactions you're feeling. It's important that you be honest with yourself when doing so. Understanding your reactions will help you determine when you're ready to share them with your partner. It will also help identify what you may still need in order to prepare sharing them.

Partner A:

_____

_____

_____

_____

_____

_____

Partner B:

_____

_____

_____

_____

_____

_____

"I Feel . . ."

Identifying your emotions, and sharing them with each other, provides an opportunity for empathy with and awareness of each other. It is important to allow for emotions that are different from each other, and to do so without judgment.

While you go through this chapter, keep in mind that both your feelings and your partner's feelings are valid. This is true regardless of how different your feelings are or how past the point of your initial intentions they may be. Attempt not to argue with your partner about their feelings. Before you respond, remember to give ownership of your feelings only to you and ownership of your partner's feelings only to them. Try using an "I feel" statement, and request that your partner do the same. How you start a conversation is important to its outcome. Don't say something accusatory like "I feel like you . . ." Instead, try "I feel the emotions you've identified."

SHARE YOUR PERCEPTION

It is easy to get stuck in the details or perceived "facts" of how a situation occurred. Remember that two people can have different perspectives on how events occurred. It's important in this part of the process to listen with the intent of understanding instead of getting stuck in whose perception is more accurate.

Now that you and your partner have shared your emotions, it's time to take turns sharing your perspective on the issue/conflict you've chosen for this chapter. Try to avoid blame and criticizing each other. Instead, share a timeline of the events of the issue much like a reporter would. Use the timeline format provided below, or develop your own, to make notes about your partner's experience, and then they will do the same for you.

After you've made your notes and developed your partner's timeline, take turns sharing your perspective. Share a summary of the notes you've taken to ensure that you've heard everything your partner has said, and that you can acknowledge it. Don't get lost on this part and argue about each detail. There can be two perspectives here, and they both deserve to be heard. You do not have to agree with each other to listen to each other.

Partner A *(These are filled out by Partner B)*

Partner B *(These are filled out by Partner A)*

Now that you have each taken turns sharing your perspectives without blame or assessing right from wrong in interpretation, it's time to pause for internal reflection. Think about how different each of you are around the same conflict. How difficult was it for you to listen and try to understand the problem from your partner's perspective? Write down your thoughts in the space provided.

Partner A: ....

....

....

....

Partner B: ....

....

....

....

continued ▸ ▸

How did writing down notes help you as opposed to just reacting to your partner's experience? Did it make it easier or more difficult for you to focus?

Partner A: _____

_____

_____

_____

_____

_____

_____

Partner B: _____

_____

_____

_____

_____

_____

_____

Practice Listening and Validating

Your partner's feelings matter. Validation provides an opportunity to share that their feelings were heard, and you heard them.

The next time you and your partner are talking about problems that have arisen from issues within the relationship or from outside stressors or events, focus on validating the emotions and summarizing your partner's facts. When you are summarizing your partner's experience is where you can use "you" statements. You want to keep your partner's experience about them, not about your thoughts on what they're saying. Remember, you don't have to agree with them; just let them know what you heard them say about their feelings and perspective.

TRIGGERS OR UNDERLYING STORIES

Beneath every perception is a story or underlying sensitivity that you and your partner perceive.

In this exercise, take turns looking at the following list of prompts. Check the box next to the prompt(s) that resonate with you, then share with your partner the story of why this may be a sensitive feeling or assumption for you. It may be based on your childhood history, past relationship(s), or ongoing issues in your current relationship. Again, you're still listening to each other and not making judgments about experiences or sensitivities.

Partner A   Partner B

☐   I felt excluded.

☐   I felt judged.

☐   I felt disrespected.

☐   I felt I had no voice at all.

☐   I felt I was powerless to fix things.

☐   I couldn't articulate or find the words to share
              what I was feeling or experiencing.

My story is valid, and it deserves to be heard.

What Is the Story You're Telling Yourself?

The stories you tell yourself about your partner or a situation will largely determine not only the emotions that come into play, but also your behaviors or reactions to the event or situation.

Get into the practice of asking yourself and your partner, "What is the story you're telling yourself?" If you understand those stories, you can better understand yourself, your partner, and how you react. This helps you make more mindful and open choices about your behaviors. Your family of origin or past relationships can shape what you see in current relationships. It's important to reflect on those stories with your partner to reduce defensiveness and take ownership of your own perception. It also leaves room for your partner to have a different story. This is where you practice listening to understand instead of listening to respond. Make it a point to implement "What is the story you're telling yourself?" this week as you work through something with your partner.

WHAT SET YOU UP?

The context around conflict can have a huge influence on your sensitivities, reaction time, and the intensity of your reaction. Letting your partner know what may be going on with you behind the scenes can help improve empathy and awareness.

While focusing on the conflict or issue you've chosen for this chapter, use the list of prompts provided to identify your state of mind at the time of the issue. Choose the prompt(s) that resonate for you around the time of the conflict, and, in the space provided, begin to develop an apology to your partner for the way it went down and for your responsibility in it. Developing an apology may be difficult, so use the space provided to collect your thoughts and write down what you want your apology to touch on. This isn't intended as a letter of apology; this is simply an area where you can write and review your notes before you give your apology.

1. I've been really stressed and easily irritated of late.

Partner A: ....

....

Partner B: ....

....

2. I haven't been sharing much of my inner world with you.

Partner A: ....

....

Partner B: ....

....

3. I've been struggling with depression lately.

Partner A: ....

....

Partner B: ....

....

4. We haven't been making time for good things between us.

Partner A: ....

....

Partner B: ....

....

5. I've been feeling unappreciated.

Partner A: ....

....

Partner B: ....

....

6. I've struggled with feelings of self-worth and not feeling good enough.

Partner A: ....

....

Partner B: ....

....

continued ▸ ▸

WHAT SET YOU UP? continued

It's important to check in with yourself about what you may be going through and how it may be impacting your mental and emotional well-being. It is very common to suffer from mental health diagnoses like depression or anxiety. You may also feel the burden of stress from day-to-day life, which can greatly impact your emotional health and your relationships.

It is normal to be afraid to be a burden or to talk to someone about what's happening with you on the inside. Take time to personally reflect on what your mental state and/or physical health has been like lately and if you need support. Use the space provided to write a self-check-in summary. How are you really doing?

Partner A:

Partner B:

The Art of a Genuine Apology

Giving a genuine apology requires empathy and an understanding of how your actions impact others. You want to share with both your tone and your words what you are accepting responsibility for. If you can't give a genuine apology, it could be because you don't believe your side is being heard. You may still be triggered or struggling with anger and feeling overwhelmed about the issue. Or you don't trust that your partner is able to take responsibility, either.

Over the next week, practice giving a genuine apology to your partner. You wrote down notes for your apology earlier in this chapter. Use those notes to help you reflect and craft a strong apology that resonates with you, rather than just apologizing to keep the peace. Once you feel like you're ready, share your apology with your partner. Sharing an apology means taking ownership for how you added to this dynamic, whether or not you were aware of it. We can't change the past or make something less hurtful. However, we can reflect and learn from the experience, take ownership, and use what we've learned to shape future interactions for the better.

MAKE A PLAN

To conclude the conversation around the conflict you've chosen for this chapter, huddle up to assemble takeaways that can help you work through a conflict like this better next time.

Work together to conduct an assessment of what you've learned, what you could use more work on, and some ground rules that you can both agree on for when conflict arises in the future. This plan should reflect everything you have learned about yourself and your partner throughout this chapter. It could be related to sharing emotions with each other, practicing not blaming, or asking each other "What is the story you're telling yourself?" Maybe it's about the tone that could be softened. Try to work together to clearly state a plan that will help both of you move forward.

What We've Learned

_____

_____

_____

_____

_____

What We Need to Work On

_____

_____

_____

_____

_____

The Ground Rules We'll Set When in Conflict

1. ....

2. ....

3. ....

4. ....

5. ....

You don't want to agree to something you know you can't follow through on. Do you ever say you'll do something even if you're not sure you can really do it? Do you do it so you can attempt to avoid disappointing your partner? Even having the best of intentions isn't enough if you lack the ability to see your promise through.

As you reflect on the plan you and your partner made from the exercise above, is there anything about the plan you worry about when it comes to your ability to follow through? Maybe you need to set clearer expectations about what you can actually deliver. It may be helpful to ask your partner how you can make a repair or communicate with them if the plan needs to change. Take time to record your thoughts below.

Partner A: ....

....

....

....

Partner B: ....

....

....

....

Identify Your Blind Spots

No matter how much you may want to do something or be good at something, you simply don't know what you don't know. Asking for feedback from trusted people in your life can help you better identify your blind spots and information gaps.

Identify a trusted person in your life—a friend, your partner, a therapist, or a family member—and ask them to give you feedback about how you show up in conflict or manage your emotions. This is an act of vulnerability on your part, so make sure it is someone you admire and respect for how they manage their lives and emotions. You need a safe person you feel comfortable sharing your emotions with. Set up a time to meet with them, tell them about what you're learning in this workbook, and explain how you'd like or need their help. This will also give you an opportunity to ask for accountability as you make changes to your communication style and identification of emotions. What you're learning in this book can often be hard to implement right away, and you will need time to practice. Having someone who knows what you're working on can help you stay engaged and motivated in the process.

KEY TAKEAWAYS

In this chapter, you walked through an entire conflict in a more structured way. You learned to understand that there are (at least) two sides to every story and that both sides are valid. Taking the time to slow down and work through conflict in a productive way can keep you from building up resentment. It can also help reduce the intensity of your triggers because you're actually working together to become aware and show up more effectively in your relationships. You can use the steps you've learned in this chapter to help walk you through any conflict in the future.

- Start by identifying your feelings. Saying your emotions out loud can help reduce the intensity with which you feel and react to them.

- Share your perception of an issue without blaming your partner. This takes time and requires really slowing down and using "I" statements.

- Using "you" statements while summarizing what you're hearing your partner say keeps it about their experience and not your own interpretation of it.

- Identify triggers and your state of mind that could be making an issue bigger than it should be.

- Work together on a plan that can help both of you handle conflicts better than you handled the one you just experienced.

CHAPTER EIGHT

Being Direct about Your Wants and Needs

It has been my experience as a marriage counselor that many times people believe that they're expressing their needs and feelings directly, and that they're at a loss as to why their partner still isn't changing or listening. The fact is, it is more about *how* you say something that will determine whether or not it is received.

It's also important to keep in mind that you or your partner may have sensitivities to being perceived a certain way, having your intentions misread, or being triggered by certain needs. Couples struggle to share their needs with each other if they come to the table with old stories about why or why not a particular need is too much or can't be met. Try to remain open-minded, with the ability to summarize and ask questions, to ensure you're interpreting and hearing each other correctly.

In this chapter, you will encounter a variety of exercises and practices to explore what your needs are, learn how to share them in a positively stated way, and identify building blocks for healthy communication.

MARK AND SIMON

Mark and Simon have been married for more than ten years, and much of what they fight about centers on emotional and physical intimacy. At some point they've tried everything—talking, planning, not talking, and seeking counseling. They felt hopeless about their ability to make things right while not giving up the things they desired and needed most in the relationship.

Personal reflection through journaling, reading books, listening to podcasts, and personal therapy helped Mark and Simon really get in touch with what their core needs were in the relationship. The couple then began to develop ritualistic time together to share those needs, review how well they were accommodating the other's needs, and determine if a compromise was necessary based on weekly events.

Mark and Simon began to focus more on what they had in common and assume positive intent with each other. That helped them go a long way toward sharing their needs and not withholding them or becoming resentful of each other. They learned that emotional and physical intimacy can happen in small ways at the same time, with both people putting in the effort and evaluating how that felt and what the next steps would be.

WRITE DOWN THE NEEDS YOU KNOW

Beginning this chapter with identifying what you know will help you gain traction on meeting needs and sharing them from a more positive perspective. This is a personal check-in for each of you.

This exercise provides you with a checklist that captures some primary needs couples have in a relationship. If a need applies to you, circle "T" for "True." If it doesn't, circle "F" for "False." As you go through the list, keep in mind that there is no good or bad choice. Without judging each other, use this exercise to talk through your feelings or stories around the need.

Partner A   **Partner B**

T   F   **1.** I need my partner to listen to my stressful events   T   F
without trying to fix anything or offer advice.

T   F   **2.** I need my partner to give me hugs, kisses, or kind   T   F
touches without expecting sex.

T   F   **3.** I need both of us to share our emotions with each   T   F
other more frequently, as a way of checking in with
how we're doing.

T   F   **4.** I need us to make time for sex on a more regular basis.   T   F

T   F   **5.** I need foreplay to be used before we move   T   F
straight to sex.

T   F   **6.** I need my partner to give me the benefit of the   T   F
doubt instead of assuming I was trying to hurt them
with what I say or share.

T   F   **7.** I need my partner to plan date nights with me at least   T   F
_____ times a month.

continued ▶ ▶

WRITE DOWN THE NEEDS YOU KNOW continued

After you've identified the needs you have from the previous exercise, write down and share with your partner the one need that feels most significant to you in this relationship right now and why. Make sure that neither of you is distracted when you have this conversation; be tuned in and listen attentively to each other. The goal is not to fix or make promises, but to practice curiosity by learning to understand why this need is so important to your partner. Take turns sharing with each other.

Partner A: My partner's greatest need right now is _____ because

_____

_____

_____

_____

_____

Partner B: My partner's greatest need right now is _____ because

_____

_____

_____

_____

_____

Daily Reflection

If you don't know what your needs are and aren't checking in with yourself daily, then you won't be able to communicate them to your partner. You may laugh and joke about your partner not being clairvoyant, but that doesn't stop you from feeling unseen if your needs aren't interpreted. Needs have to be known and shared frequently. Even the same needs have to be shared more than once.

Set time aside during your daily commute to work or while you're doing a workout, or journal daily to connect with yourself and identify what your needs for the relationship may be for the day, the week, or the month. When you check in with your partner at the end of the day, you can share your needs with them. You can practice this daily check-in by asking yourself questions like "How am I feeling in my relationship today?" or "Do I have needs or expectations for my partner that I haven't shared?" Also, consider asking yourself how you may be able to meet some of your own needs.

HOW TO IDENTIFY A NEED

What you practice is what you will use in times of conflict. The same is true when it comes to identifying your needs. You need to identify your needs before you can reasonably expect to have your needs met.

Make a point of using this format with your partner, on a daily basis, to get in the habit of identifying and sharing your needs and feelings with each other. These tools are referred to by the Gottman Institute as the "Softened Start-Up."

1. **"I feel . . ."** : Review the following list of emotions and choose one.

Example: "I feel defensive . . ."

Partner A: ....

Partner B: ....

Accused	Concerned	Heard	Sad
Affectionate	Connected	Hopeful	Seen
Angry	Defensive	Lonely	Stressed
Attacked	Exhausted	Loved	Valued
Close	Frustrated	Resentful	Worried

2. **"About what . . ."** : Explain where those emotions are coming from with-out blaming your partner or using "you" statements.

Example: " . . . when my actions are interpreted as if I don't care or that I'm not listening."

Partner A: ....

....

Partner B: ....

....

3. **"I need . . ."** : Think about the emotion that you chose earlier. If it was a more "negative" emotion, what would be its positive opposite? If it was a more "positive" emotion, what would maintain that positivity toward your partner?

Example: "I need for you to summarize what you hear me say so I know it's being interpreted the way it was intended, and for you to ask me questions if you don't understand."

Partner A: ....

....

....

Partner B: ....

....

....

continued ▸ ▸

Talk with your partner about some of the emotions they express that are more off-putting to you. For example, you may be really sensitive and automatically shut down if your partner says they're angry with you. You may respond more positively if they share a positive emotion of what they *want* to feel as opposed to what they *do* feel.

Write down the emotions that your partner shares with you, then circle the up arrow if it's a positive emotion that's expressed, or the down arrow if it's a negative emotion. Review the lists together and discuss.

PARTNER A EMOTIONS: *(These are filled out by Partner B)*	POSITIVE	NEGATIVE
1.	▲	▼
2.	▲	▼
3.	▲	▼
4.	▲	▼
5.	▲	▼

PARTNER B EMOTIONS: *(These are filled out by Partner A)*		
1.	▲	▼
2.	▲	▼
3.	▲	▼
4.	▲	▼
5.	▲	▼

Emotion Identification

Your emotions are what drive your needs and responses. If you're feeling overwhelmed, angry, defensive, or sad, it is best to name your emotion before you react.

Naming your emotions tames them and gives you information about what to do next. Try to slow down, take a deep breath, and ask yourself, "What emotion am I feeling right now?" before responding, reacting, or sharing with your partner. This can be a more challenging exercise if you have a limited emotional vocabulary or find that you are often feeling overwhelmed or angry. Try taking yourself a little deeper into your emotional experience by using an emotional vocabulary chart that you find online. If you are having difficulty locating one, consult the Resources section at the back of this book.

WHY IS THIS NEED SO IMPORTANT TO ME?

There are stories underneath every need. Some of these stories might come from your childhood, past relationships, or even your current relationship. These stories that you consciously or unconsciously tell yourself can affect the way you share your needs or even why you don't share them.

   For this exercise, choose the needs that are most important to you and fill in the blanks. You can do this by reading the prompt out loud with your partner or by writing it down to share with them later.

1. It's important to me to share my feelings and stressful experiences with my partner without them trying to fix or offer advice because . . .

Partner A:

Partner B:

2. I need my partner to touch and kiss me without the follow-through of sex because . . .

Partner A:

Partner B:

3. When my partner shares their emotions with me more frequently, it helps me to . . .

Partner A:

Partner B:

4. Having sex with my partner more regularly is important to me because . . .

Partner A: _____

_____

Partner B: _____

_____

5. Spending more time in foreplay as opposed to just skipping straight to sex matters to me because . . .

Partner A: _____

_____

Partner B: _____

_____

6. My partner assuming my intentions as positive is important to me because . . .

Partner A: _____

_____

Partner B: _____

_____

My needs are important in all my relationships.

Daily Practice of Sharing Your Emotions and Needs

Whatever you practice daily will eventually be what comes natural in times of conflict. If your practice is to not share your thoughts and feelings, you will find it really hard to do so when it becomes necessary. If you practice sharing your needs in the form of criticism, that is how you will start a conflict that will eventually lead to nowhere, and both you and your partner will feel hurt and angry.

Every day, in some small way, practice sharing with your partner through a softened start-up. Remember, a softened start-up consists of language like "I feel," "about," and "I need." Your daily practice with each other can be over coffee, dinner, or texts, and it doesn't have to be about a conflict. It can go something like "I feel really excited about my upcoming work project, and I need to spend a few minutes tonight putting the outline together."

CORE NEEDS VS. FLEXIBLE NEEDS

Eventually you and your partner need to move from sharing your needs with each other to active problem-solving, especially if you each have very different needs. What often happens is that partners tend to focus more on how different they are than on how alike. A core need is something you absolutely must have so that you don't feel like you're giving up a piece of yourself or something that is really important to you. Flexible needs differ from core needs in that they can adapt to the issue at hand and won't cause built-up resentment if they aren't met. For example, you may have a core need of having a fixed budget to adhere to, while your flexible need may be around when you sit down to look over your finances to prepare to make a budget.

In the circles provided, write your core needs in the smaller circles around a topic that you decide on as a couple. It could be about chores for the coming weekend or scheduling date nights. In the larger circles, write what you're flexible about. Once you've each spent time filling out your circles, explain what your core needs are and why they're important to you. Do this without judgment. You will then share your areas of flexibility and what those flexible areas look like. This will help you begin the process of seeing where you are alike in the flexible areas.

The goal of moving forward together is taking one small or temporary step forward while still honoring the core needs of each partner. Make the small or temporary step forward come from your flexible areas.

Partner A   **Partner B**

continued ▸▸

CORE NEEDS VS. FLEXIBLE NEEDS continued

Referring to the core and flexible needs you wrote down in the previous exercise, speak together about what you noticed that you agreed on. It helps to focus on where you are alike when trying to make some headway on a difficult topic. Instead of becoming mired in your differences, try to emphasize how you are somewhat similar and work together. Write down your common goals below so they're available whenever you or your partner need a reminder.

1. _____

2. _____

3. _____

4. _____

5. _____

6. _____

7. _____

8. _____

9. _____

10. _____

Solvable vs. Perpetual

Each of you brings a certain set of issues into a relationship. There is no perfect relationship out there, because everyone is different. Your approaches to conflict, money, sex, children, and chores may never be 100 percent alike.

Work to get in the habit of recognizing when an issue is solvable and when it may be an ongoing issue that you have to constantly talk about because of how different you are. You can easily decide where you are going for dinner tonight, but you may not be so easily able to determine how best you and your partner should spend your money.

The next time a conflict comes up, ask yourself, and each other, if this issue is something that can be solved, or if it hits deeper issues that you struggle to work through. If it's solvable, then solve it. If it's perpetual, go back through the tools of the softened start-up, speaker/listener roles, and sharing core needs versus flexible needs to come up with a temporary or partial step forward. The easiest way to identify whether an issue is solvable or not is to gauge your reactions. If you find that this is a topic you and your partner avoid or tend to go round and round in circles about, it's probably an insoluble perpetual issue that you will need to learn tools for dialoguing about.

SELF-ASSESSMENT AROUND COMPROMISE

Healthy compromise is the ability to identify and honor each other's core needs and concentrate more on your areas of flexibility, to make temporary or small steps forward. You may have to make many compromises around the same topic throughout your relationship because of your differences.

Review the following statements and take this opportunity to self-assess if you're truly all right with the compromises you've made or feel like you have to make by circling either "T" for "True" or "F" for "False." This assessment will help you identify if you and your partner need to revisit some issues or have a serious conversation around a topic you have yet to explore.

Partner A   **Partner B**

T F   **1.** I feel like I've let go of my core needs to stay in   T F
             the relationship.

T F   **2.** I have resentment toward my partner that I can't   T F
             let go of.

T F   **3.** I am able to talk to my partner about my core   T F
             needs and feelings.

As you reflect on the issues in your relationship, talk together without judgment, blame, or defensiveness about the issues you feel you two have tried to tackle without the help of a therapist or mentor that aren't going anywhere. Or talk about issues you have that you haven't tried to share before because you may be worried or don't feel like you can share them.

Discuss how you can each incorporate some of the tools you've learned so far in this book, or ask how open each of you may be to getting counseling support to talk about certain issues. Resources for getting in touch with counselors in your area are included in the Resources section of this workbook. To help you focus on the areas you want to address, write down the issues that you need professional support with. Be sure to not only include what you think discussing these issues will most help you with, but also identify how it may help your relationship with your partner.

Partner A:

Partner B:

Make It Consistent

Whether you need to seek support from a counselor to discuss difficult issues or you want to try out the resources you've learned in this book, make sure that you set aside consistent time to do it.

Start with weekly times on the calendar at home or in a clinician's office. You aren't trying to fix all of your problems at once, so if you try to talk something through and things get heated, just take a break and commit to trying again the following week.

The goal is to learn how to communicate, not become excellent communicators and problem-solvers overnight. Reflect on how this is a long-term strategy for better understanding yourselves and each other as opposed to just fixing one issue and moving on. With practice and consistency, you will find that topics that once caused you to want to pull your hair out or avoid altogether become topics that you can now talk through, understand why they're important to you, and identify what your specific needs may be.

KEY TAKEAWAYS

Learning to share your wants and needs takes self-awareness, practice, and intention. No couple becomes expert communicators with each other overnight. You build awareness and vulnerability with practice and trust.

Here are several other key items to remember from this chapter:

- Make time to reflect on what your current needs are in this relationship. Share them from the perspective of what you want to have happen as opposed to a viewpoint of what you don't want to have happen.

- Your needs often stem from your emotions. It's important to practice identifying your feelings with more descriptive emotional vocabulary so you can be clearer about the emotion you'd like to experience.

- The first three minutes of a conversation often dictate how that conversation will end. Start a conflict with a softened start-up: "I feel (insert emotion) about (why that emotion is present without blaming)," and "I need (share what you want instead of what you don't want)."

- Get a sense of what needs you must have met on an important topic (core need) that you can't go without, then focus on what you're willing to talk about or work through more (flexibility).

- Get good at focusing on where you are alike and making small steps forward there knowing that you will have to keep coming back and talking.

CHAPTER NINE

Establishing Healthy Boundaries

Setting healthy boundaries is important, but what does it actually mean? In this chapter, you will focus on defining healthy boundaries, learning your natural responses to setting boundaries, and how to set them. The hard part about setting boundaries is that if you have never set them before, you're likely to feel nervous or guilty about it. Many people will struggle with you learning to set boundaries because they've been used to you not having any. You especially have to be careful in the way you set and share them within your romantic relationship with your partner.

Healthy boundary setting will change your life and relationships, and it will teach you very quickly which relationships in your life are worth dedicating your energy to.

TONY AND STEFAN

Tony and Stefan had been together since high school. They described their relationship as easy and fulfilling until sex started becoming a really big topic of discussion. Tony began to shut down emotionally when they even talked about having sex. Not wanting to push or upset his partner, Stefan often didn't share her feelings or requests for intimacy. After several years of having issues around sex, the couple began to fight and experience bitterness toward each other for their needs not being met and what felt like their boundaries being crossed.

After starting couples therapy together, Tony was diagnosed with post-traumatic stress disorder from trauma he experienced in early childhood. With the guidance and education of their counselor, the couple identified that the issues around intimacy largely stemmed from Tony's past experiences. Tony and Stefan eventually learned how to talk about their boundaries around communicating and having intimacy. They worked out what was all right and what was off-limits and how to handle an issue if a trigger came up. Months later, the couple is having sex more regularly and sharing openly with each other about what is working in their relationship and what is not.

BOUNDARY CHECK-IN

This is a little check-in to get your initial thoughts on boundaries before you jump into the nitty-gritty details of setting them with your partner.

Circle "True" or "False" in reaction to the following statements. After you're both done, use your answers to spur your thoughts on boundaries with each other. You may notice that you're more alike than you thought.

1. I can easily define what a boundary is.

Partner A:	True	False
Partner B:	True	False

2. I feel really confident in setting boundaries with my partner.

Partner A:	True	False
Partner B:	True	False

3. I often feel guilty when I set boundaries with my partner.

Partner A:	True	False
Partner B:	True	False

4. My partner responds well to my boundaries.

Partner A:	True	False
Partner B:	True	False

5. I often hear from my partner that my boundaries are "too much."

Partner A:	True	False
Partner B:	True	False

continued ▸ ▸

BOUNDARY CHECK-IN continued

Take a moment to write down your own definition of what a boundary is. Even if you're unsure about how to define it, give it a try. Don't look up the answer online; think about your own experiences with boundaries.

After both of you have written down your answers, discuss them and notice how different or alike your definitions are. Remember, no judgments. This is about open and honest communication between two people who care about each other.

Partner A: A boundary is . . .

_____

_____

_____

_____

Partner B: A boundary is . . .

_____

_____

_____

_____

Knowing When to Set a Boundary

Sometimes you may not realize you have a boundary until you think that one has been crossed. Oftentimes, your boundaries may look like expectations, and you won't know they were missed until you have the feeling of being taken advantage of, unheard, or overwhelmed.

Over the next few days, take note when you have negative feelings toward your partner. Ask yourself, "Is this feeling coming from a missed expectation or lack of follow-through?"

Here's an example: You come home from work, and the house is a mess. Your partner has been home all day and didn't bother cleaning up. You start huffing and puffing while you clean up the house and feel a lot of anger toward your partner. This would be an example of a boundary/expectation that needs to be set. When you feel upset at or resentful toward your partner, it is generally a sign you aren't setting healthy and clear boundaries with them.

HEALTHY BOUNDARY IDENTIFICATION

After talking through boundaries with your partner, you are likely to find that your definitions of boundaries are pretty similar. They are likely to center on what is and isn't acceptable about a situation or interaction.

In the following grid, take turns writing down one issue that you have together as a couple. Below the issue, write down what is and is not acceptable about the situation. For this exercise, it's important to use and agree on the same issue/situation. Boundaries take time to work on and work up to. Try starting with a smaller issue for this exercise and familiarize yourself with how to use this concept. Remember, the only thing you're attempting to do in this exercise is to identify what is and is not acceptable, to get in the habit of asking yourself these questions before communicating with your partner.

The Issue:
Example: You come home from work, and the house is a mess even though your partner has been home all day.

Partner A

ACCEPTABLE	NOT ACCEPTABLE
Example: Getting some rest on your day off; not needing to be thorough, just cleaned up	Agreeing to clean up and not following through on the promise

ACCEPTABLE	NOT ACCEPTABLE
Example: Want to come home to a clean house; asking for help	Harsh tone and high expectations with little collaboration; only focusing on what didn't get done vs. what did get done

When you think about setting boundaries, do you notice that it is harder to identify what is okay about a situation than what is not okay about it? It's important to remember that focusing only on what you don't want doesn't help you identify what you *do* want, nor does it account for the feelings, needs, and differing perceptions of others.

Discuss with your partner how sharing what is or isn't okay about a situation might help both of you communicate without criticism and defensiveness toward each other. In the space provided, write down one example of sharing what you want when it comes to sharing boundaries with each other.

Partner A: _____

_____

_____

Partner B: _____

_____

_____

Try Sharing a Boundary

Setting boundaries has to become intentional as a way of staying mindful of your promises to yourself and educating others on how to love and show up for you best.

At some point this week, schedule a time to sit down and talk with each other for about five to ten minutes. Come prepared to discuss an issue that came up between the two of you this week and share what about it was acceptable and what wasn't, for each of you. Set a timer for no more than ten minutes to end the conversation so that it doesn't get heated.

Remember, practicing boundaries takes time. Be gentle with yourself and your partner as each of you attempt to practice identifying and setting boundaries with each other. Setting aside a regular time to talk about issues in your relationship leads to fewer blowups, more engagement in each other's inner world, healthier expectations of core issues, and follow-through when it comes to meeting needs in the relationship.

I FEEL GUILTY WHEN . . .

When first beginning boundary work, the most common emotion a person experiences is guilt. Guilt can have a tendency to keep you silent, and when you stay silent you are more apt to build resentment. Boundaries are a guide to teach others how to love and treat you. If someone doesn't know your boundaries, then they are missing a piece of the puzzle to loving you better.

Use the spaces provided to write down a boundary you feel the guiltiest for having, or for wanting to share with your partner. After you've taken the brave step of writing it down, continue by sharing it out loud with your partner. Discuss what each of you wrote, without judgment.

Example: "I feel guilty for setting a boundary regarding having sex during the week because I know you want to be spontaneous, but I lack energy and can't be fully present."

Partner A: I feel guilty for setting a boundary regarding _____

because _____ .

Partner B: I feel guilty for setting a boundary regarding _____

because _____ .

*Setting healthy boundaries is a way to teach
my partner how to love me better.*

Driving Emotions

Your emotions often drive your behaviors and reactions. If you're not setting boundaries, it is because you have stronger emotions that keep you from doing so, or your emotions are causing your boundaries to be very fixed.

Take a moment with your partner to share an emotion that often drives whether or not you share a boundary with your partner and how you might end up sharing it. Also share with your partner the emotion you'd like to drive boundary setting. For example: "I might share a boundary when I'm really angry, and instead of sharing calmly I will yell at my partner and talk down to them. I'd rather share my boundaries with my partner from a place of calm and trust that it's okay to have and set boundaries." Shame, fear, and/or guilt can keep you from sharing your boundaries with your partner because you don't want to be too much and end up losing or hurting the relationship. Keep in mind that having boundaries helps enhance the health of a relationship because it is teaching others how to love you best.

VERBAL VS. NONVERBAL BOUNDARIES

We often think of boundaries as something we communicate verbally to another person. But boundaries can also be shared nonverbally by refusing to engage, walking away, or not responding. You get to decide what you give energy to. When you share a boundary verbally, it can require energy and an active dialogue. You and your partner may have different perceptions on how to handle the sharing or setting of a boundary, and that's fine.

In the space provided, you will practice identifying when a boundary can be shared verbally or nonverbally by checking the box that resonates with the response you'd give. After each of you has checked off your answers, use this as an opportunity to discuss why each of you chose your responses and how you might approach a situation verbally or nonverbally (depending on your answer).

1. My partner makes a joke that I don't think is funny.   ☐ ☐ A   ☐ ☐ B

2. My partner spends money when we agreed not to.   ☐ ☐ A   ☐ ☐ B

3. My partner tries to initiate sex when I'm not in the mood.   ☐ ☐ A   ☐ ☐ B

4. My partner doesn't help with the chores around the house.   ☐ ☐ A   ☐ ☐ B

5. My partner agrees to plans with others without checking with me first.   ☐ ☐ A   ☐ ☐ B

6. I'm exhausted, and my partner wants to talk about something I don't have the energy for.   ☐ ☐ A   ☐ ☐ B

7. I'm irritated, stressed, or otherwise occupied, and my partner is trying to show physical affection.   ☐ ☐ A   ☐ ☐ B

continued ▶▶

VERBAL VS. NONVERBAL BOUNDARIES continued

Think back to an occasion when you shared a boundary verbally with your partner and how you believe it went. Next, think of a time when you shared a nonverbal boundary with your partner and how that went.

Write down and share those experiences with your partner without blame or returning it to an old argument. Ask each other how these boundaries could be shared differently in the future that would make them go better, or share what about them went well the first time.

Partner A

Shared a verbal boundary: _____

_____

Next time: _____

_____

Shared a nonverbal boundary: _____

_____

Next time: _____

_____

Partner B

Shared a verbal boundary: _____

_____

Next time: _____

_____

Shared a nonverbal boundary: _____

_____

Next time: _____

_____

Move Past Guilt

Guilt is a natural reaction to making a mistake. Feeling guilty when it comes to setting a boundary comes from a desire to please.

This week, if you notice yourself feeling guilty about wanting to share or establish a boundary, tell yourself the following statement: "Feeling guilty over setting a boundary is a sign I need to grow and press on with setting the boundary."

Having a mantra will keep you focused on what you're trying to accomplish instead of getting stuck in old patterns. You will need a lot of practice with boundary setting, and be sure to construct a boundary thinking about what is and is not okay about the situation you're setting it for. Mantras are also a grounding tool for staying true to yourself. Take some time to think about and write down what your mantra might be around boundaries, and keep it somewhere handy like your phone or journal that you can read and reflect on frequently.

FLEXIBLE VS. INFLEXIBLE BOUNDARIES

Depending on your relationship with boundaries and the state of your romantic relationship, your boundaries may need to become firmer, or in some cases, less firm. When couples don't share boundaries, they aren't teaching each other how to best be loved. When a person's boundaries are very black-and-white, they leave little room for compromise that honors the needs of both people.

Work together to assemble a list of the main issues in your relationship right now.

1. ....
2. ....
3. ....
4. ....
5. ....
6. ....
7. ....
8. ....
9. ....
10. ....

★ Draw a star next to the topics you and your partner trust each other to figure out together. Your boundaries are generally more flexible when you trust each other to hear your point of view and work together to solve the issues.

✓ Next to the topics you were unable to star, place a check mark. These may be areas where you and your partner have very different views and have a difficult time talking about them. You may need to slow down the problem-solving and focus on the other communication tools you've learned in this book, such as speaker/listener roles, softened start-up, and expressing needs, before you move to active boundary setting.

The two of you have learned a lot in this chapter about your reactions to and feelings about boundaries. You have identified topics in your relationship that you can talk about and work through and topics that you can't.

Talk to each other about the tools you've learned in this chapter that you'd like to try at home. Also discuss if you need outside support from a counselor, coach, or mentor. Decide what your next step will be here, so you can see some progress moving forward related to boundary setting. Use the lines provided to write down, in order, what your next steps will be. Create the steps together and ensure that both of you are on the same page.

1. ....

2. ....

3. ....

4. ....

5. ....

6. ....

Make a Commitment

Taking the time to tell each other what you've learned and what you're going to commit to doing helps each of you to stay aware of your partner's attempts to make things better in the relationship.

Share with your partner your biggest takeaway from this chapter on boundaries. Next, share one thing you will commit to putting into practice. Be specific with how you're going to keep it top of mind and when you are going to practice it with your partner so they can be on the lookout. When you see your partner trying to follow through, make sure to share an appreciation of their attempts.

Accountability is important to staying the course in what you've promised yourself you'll do. Our partner is also learning at the same time. Being each other's source of accountability should be fun and helpful. Remember, it's not about using each other's promise to do something to shame them for not doing it. You two are collaborating and working together to build the relationship that you desire. Sharing feedback with kindness and gentleness in tone (not when you're upset) will support both of you in following through.

KEY TAKEAWAYS

Boundaries are a tough topic to tackle. Congratulate yourself and your partner for making your way through extensive exercises, prompts, and practices that help you understand what boundaries are, plus when and how to share them, and for identifying emotions that can hinder you from sharing your boundaries.

Highlights from this chapter include:

- Having a lack of boundaries comes from a desire to please others.

- Having black-and-white boundaries is a sign of trust issues in a relationship that showcase the need for additional support from a therapist, coach, or mentor.

- Boundaries can be shared both verbally and nonverbally by asking yourself, "Do I want to give energy to this right now?"

- Learning to set boundaries will often bring up a sense of guilt or dread. That is not a sign that you shouldn't set the boundary. It is a sign that you should move forward on setting it.

- When it comes to sharing your boundaries, start with what about the issue or situation is acceptable. Then move on to what is not acceptable and what your partner can do to make it right. Sharing what is okay is a way of honoring another person and recognizing they have feelings, needs, and a different perspective.

- Share boundaries when you are calm and have had time to think through what it is you really need.

- Communicate with your partner about your desire to better understand their boundaries as well. Set aside time weekly to discuss what went well this week when it came to boundaries and what could have gone better.

- Boundaries take time to practice and to get used to. Be patient with yourselves and each other as you work on creating them.

A FINAL NOTE

What a journey you have been on together! You have a lot to be proud of as you come to the conclusion of this workbook. Building and sustaining a healthy relationship takes time, effort, and consistency.

Together, you've learned that healthy communication relies heavily on empathy, on the desire to listen, and on how you share yourself with your partner. You can communicate about anything when you know how to communicate. That starts with a willingness to learn about each other's differences, share experiences from your lives, and create a relationship that feels unique to the two of you.

Feel free to return to the chapters and exercises you've learned in this book as often as you need to. Creating a new way of communicating will take a lot of practice. It's easy to get discouraged if progress takes time or if one or both partners is struggling to use the tools. Evaluate together if you need additional support from a therapist, coach, or mentor, and make sure it's someone you both trust. Be careful who you share information about your relationship with, and have trusted people you both can count on when you need it.

RESOURCES

Books

Come as You Are: The Surprising New Science That Will Transform Your Sex Life by Emily Nagoski
This book offers in-depth insight into female sexuality and how to better connect with yourself and your partner. For all couples wanting to increase their understanding of sexuality, this is a great read to do separately or apart.

Couples Money: What Every Couple Should Know about Money and Relationships by Marlow and Chris Felton
This book provides great insight and discussion about the differences that couples can have about money and how to talk about it.

Hold Me Tight: Seven Conversations for a Lifetime of Love by Sue Johnson
Sue Johnson is the creator of emotionally focused therapy, which is designed to support clinicians and couples in assessing for and treating issues related to attachment. Healthy attachment is all about how we express our needs and how we respond to the needs of our partner.

Love Sense: The Revolutionary New Science of Romantic Relationships by Sue Johnson
If you love research and want to understand how the brain responds to love and trust, look no further. This book reviews research from the past century into how we connect with others, what keeps us connected, or what tears us apart.

Magnificent Sex: Lessons from Extraordinary Lovers by Peggy J. Kleinplatz and A. Dana Ménard
In the largest research study ever done about what makes sex so amazing, the author and her partners study thousands of people from all walks of life to find out the principles for having a great sex life.

The Seven Principles for Making Marriage Work by John M. Gottman and Nan Silver
This book offers detailed insights into the Gottman Institute's more than forty years of research done with couples to showcase how to build and maintain a healthy relationship.

***Shameless: A Case for Not Feeling Bad about Feeling Good (about Sex)* by Nadia Bolz-Weber**
Have you suffered from religious shame regarding sex, and it still impacts your relationship with yourself and your partner? This book takes you on a tour through the Bible from the perspective of a pastor working to end shame in the religious community.

***What Makes Love Last? How to Build Trust and Avoid Betrayal* by John Gottman and Nan Silver**
The research in this book expounds on what we've learned in recent decades about how relationships evolve and what eventually leads to their end. If you want to know how to make love last throughout a lifetime, this is a book for you.

Online

Tom Drummond's "Vocabulary of Emotions/Feelings." tomdrummond.com/ wp-content/uploads/2019/11/ Emotion-Feelings.pdf
This emotional vocabulary sheet is one I use every day in practice because of how comprehensive and user-friendly it is. I recommended printing it out and having it near an area where you journal or have conversations with your partner.

GottmanReferralNetwork.com
The Gottman Method is a highly specialized area of study for clinicians that want to work with couples. This website is a list of all therapists trained or certified in the Gottman Method close to you.

Marriage.com
This is an informational site with content creators who are experts in the field of marriage and family therapy. There are hundreds of blogs on the site about a variety of topics that impact couples with practical tips and tools.

PsychologyToday.com
This is a great resource for finding counselors in your area based on specialty. If you need to use someone on your insurance panel, make sure to contact your insurance company directly for a list of names.

Podcasts

Black Love Matters

Couples Therapy with Naomi Ekperigin and Andy Beckerman

Dateable with Julie Krafchick and Yue Xu

Dear Sugars

The Endless Honeymoon Podcast with Moshe Kasher and Natasha Leggero

I Do Podcast

Love, Happiness, and Success with Dr. Lisa Marie Bobby

Love Letters with Meredith Goldstein

Modern Love

Paired by the People

Savage Lovecast with Dan Savage

Where Should We Begin? with Esther Perel

REFERENCES

Brown, Brené. *Braving the Wilderness: The Quest for True Belonging and the Courage to Stand Alone*. New York: Random House, 2017.

Gottman, John M., and Nan Silver. *The Seven Principles for Making Marriage Work*. New York: Harmony Books, 2015.

Johnson, Sue. *Love Sense: The Revolutionary New Science of Romantic Relationships*. New York: Little, Brown and Company, 2013.

INDEX

Acknowledgments

I'd like to thank my amazing editor, Mike McAvennie, for helping this project come to life! The amazing designers and team at Callisto Media work tirelessly to bring amazing content to people around the world. It's been an extraordinary experience to work with all of you!

About the Author

Sonya Jensen, LMFT, is a licensed marriage and family therapist and certified Gottman Method couples and sex therapist. A leader in her field with extensive, specialized training, Sonya brings genuine heart and warmth to her practice, making her advice for couples especially accessible. In addition to having worked with couples for nearly ten years, Sonya is an author, speaker, and sought-after trainer. A candid voice for relationship health, Sonya believes that all people are worthy of a healthy, loving partnership, and she's here to be their guide.

CPSIA information can be obtained
at www.ICGtesting.com
Printed in the USA
JSHW060150221022
31855JS00011B/30